IT'S ALL BULLSHIT
One Man's Interpretation Of The Complexities Of Life
By Jeremiah Dotson

ACKNOWLEDGEMENTS

Thank you God for allowing me to publish my ninth book.
Thank you to everybody who has supported my efforts.
Thank you to all the cheap bastards who are still waiting for a free copy.
Thank you Kathy for your love.
Mark & Corey, love ya much.

Topics Of Discussion

The most beautiful thing about life is that everybody has freedom. They have the freedom to eat whatever they want, sleep whenever they want and what I believe to be the most important, think however they want. When it comes to thinking, everybody has a different interpretation or perspective on things than everybody else. There is one thing however which I believe that people the world over can come together in total agreement on and that is what is interpreted as bullshit.

When most people hear or think of the word bullshit, their minds automatically go to negative side of the spectrum believing that whatever is labeled bullshit is something that is generally untrue. An example of this would be someone working a minimum wage job and being able to afford a two hundred thousand dollar vehicle. The appropriate response to that would be bullshit. Most logical people know that there is no way in heaven or hell that an individual would be able to afford something of that magnitude on that salary so bullshit is more or less a way of quickly contradicting the obvious lie perpetrated by the other. But the term bullshit also encompasses things, which are generally not right. An example of this is how there are differences in pay when it comes to gender for the same type of employment. Another example of this is how there is a supposed glass ceiling when it comes to certain races and certain positions. And yet another example of what can aptly be described as bullshit is what public assistance gives to individuals and families to live on while they are between jobs. Most people have gone through situations, whether they were alone or whether they were with friends, which have left them either thinking or saying this is some real bullshit. Now, as we know bullshit is not just what comes out of a bull's ass. Bullshit is the complete absence of common sense. It is the epitome of nonsense. It is what people do when they do not have the correct answer. As stated above, it is what people interpret as untruthful or just not right. The term bullshitting is given to people who do not focus or who are not focusing on an objective or goal. Others will say you're bullshitting, instead of you're doing what you're supposed to be doing. For the purpose of this book, the term bullshit will be used to describe things, which fall under the just ain't right or things that just don't make any conceptual type of sense category.

And so we begin,

On Life

First let me say that when it comes to life and being alive, I do not consider either of those things to be bullshit. In fact I think that they are the best things an individual can experience. What I do consider to be an extreme level of bullshit is the way in which many people interpret them. People are much divided when it comes to the reasons for their existence. For one I have noticed that many people believe their only purpose in life is to make as much money as they can. I have also noticed that some people believe that their only purpose on earth is to live as good a life as they can to secure a favorable position in the afterlife. **Now here comes the bullshit.** <u>There is no textbook protocol on how life should be lived.</u> I mean if you want to go the religious route, then there are several religious manuals, which will help you do so. These manuals will provide massive insight on how people of certain religious beliefs should structure their way of living. But the downside to those types of teachings is that each religion has a different way in which to achieve the desired goal. For those who are not that religious, there is the idea that everyone has a vocation or purpose to fill while they are alive. Now when it comes to having a purpose in life, there are some people who will argue that the purpose of some people in this world is to be lessons to other people. In other words, these people are either the ones who excel and become rich beyond all reasonable expectation or those who become homeless or permanently incarcerated. And people who use them as lessons believe that they should either emulate them or do everything in their power to avoid ending up like them. There are others who believe that when it comes to being alive, there are certain rules you have to follow, for instance, you have to eat healthy and work out so that you can live your longest and healthiest life possible - while on the other side of the spectrum, many people believe that everything is predetermined, in other words, you are going to die at a certain time and in a certain manner, so no matter how many push ups you do or how many salads you eat, it really won't matter. When it is your time to go, it will be your time to go and no one will be able to save you. This brings up the interesting argument of who's right when it comes to why we are here and what if any is our purpose? On the side of the religious people, and their religions, there are so many of them and each one it seems, has a different method to achieving either happiness or some higher plane of existence. On the side of the non religious people, it seems that each of them have their own individual method to achieving happiness as well. And these methods are anything from working for themselves to living a life of public assistance collecting and not working at all. So then is it safe to assume that if there is a universal purpose in life, it is the one of being happy? I think so.

When you look at the big picture, the average person will be able to find some facet of bullshit in almost every aspect of life. Aside from the twenty eight topics of bullshit, which are explained in the pages that follow, there are an immeasurable number of things, which people go through daily, which they will classify as bullshit. I mean everything from the 'routine' traffic stop because you didn't come to a complete stop at a stop sign, to the boss having an argument with his wife and taking it out on you just because he can. People love to dispute some of the things I consider bullshit as necessary but here's my argument: if things are necessary, there would be no chance at classifying them as bullshit. Here's a for instance: when it comes to stopping at stop signs, this is not necessary. This is bullshit and here's my proof: I live in New York City. This city reportedly has more than eight million people living here. And many of those eight million people own cars. Now I have checked extensively and exhaustively but I have been unable to find an accurate number of how many cars there are traveling around this city at any given moment but the most agreed upon number is at least three million vehicles. Now let's say for a moment that this assumption was correct. With all of the stop signs in this city, if even half of those cars were on the road on any particular day and they obeyed this bullshit law of actually having to come to a complete stop at every stop sign, this city would come close to a standstill. Think about it, if there were four cars traveling down a particular street one behind each other, and there was a stop sign at the corner, every car would have to stop, not only at the stop sign but also whenever the car in front stopped for the stop sign. This would mean that the car in the fourth position would have to stop at least four times before he even gets to the stop sign. Now multiply that by all the stop signs in the city that this poor sap probably has to pass before he makes it to his destination. He would have road rage like a motherfucker by the time he gets there.

On top of that there are all of the people who try to sneak between the cars as they wait at the stop sign to make sure the road is clear before proceeding. And on top of that there will more than likely be some dumb dick, over zealous and under paid cop just waiting to give you a ticket because you did not come to a complete fucking stop. That's some bullshit. Before I took my driving test, I remember I was instructed to stop before I reached the stop sign, then pull up to the stop sign, make sure that no cars were coming, and then proceed. And I believe that this is how most people were taught as well. Now that people have licenses, those rules are all but forgotten. The police officers know this and not only do they know this, they figure that since almost everybody is going to ignore this rule, we can make it a crime to do so – and in the process collect gazillions of dollars in bullshit ass fines! Somebody tell me where this bullshit is necessary.

On another bullshit note, there is this thing about individuals stealing or purchasing guns and then transporting them to the inner city and either selling them to bad people or using them to commit crimes. The reason why I say this is bullshit is because I believe that people have the resources to stop this from occurring. I believe that if gun manufacturers were to install a global positioning satellite in all of the guns which are all of the guns, which are manufactured from today on, the issue of people being killed and wounded from out of state, stolen guns would be non existent. Think about it; if somebody steals a cell phone, there is technology, which will basically lead law enforcement officials almost right to the exact location of the stolen phone. There is technology, which will locate lost dogs. There is even technology, which will locate a city bus. So why can't there be the same technology on a nine millimeter? I have an Iphone and I love this phone to death. I also have a gun. I for some reason or other would be more concerned if my gun was stolen than my Iphone and here's the reason why: the gun can kill many people in a relatively short amount of time. The Iphone can't. Think about something else: if a gun is stolen and it is reported, chances are that the gun will remain missing until it is either found by luck or by someone calling in an anonymous tip or until it is used in the commission of a crime. And unfortunately, the most often way a gun is found is during or after the commission of a crime. If law enforcement knew where all of the guns were, and all of the criminals knew that law enforcement knew where all of the guns were, there would be an astronomical drop in gun related crime. This is what people don't seem t understand. There is this argument about registered gun owners versus those who carry illegal guns but I don't think that there's even an argument because registered gun owners are not the ones shooting up everybody all will nilly and shit. Illegal gun owners are the ones shooting up everybody. This is the type of technology, which is necessary. I mean finding a lost Iphone or Ipad is cool but is there any comparison at all when it comes to preventing a death or injury from a stolen weapon? I think not.

There is a lot of bullshit in other things too, such as favoritism when it comes to employment and there is even bullshit in death, starting with the sometimes astronomical prices of funerals. There is bullshit in the division of assets, from family to the people who the deceased was sleeping with. The reason why I say that all of these things are bullshit is because it is almost impossible for people to come to an amicable agreement in everything. The only thing that I have noticed that is not complete and utter bullshit is the fact that everybody in this world wants to be happy. The only problem with this is the fact that as stated above, there is no one path to attain that happiness which will work for everybody. When people attempt to find or secure happiness of their own based on what has worked for others, they are often embarking on a path of bullshit.

On Cars

Here's an interesting tidbit that many people, except for those that drive, don't realize. Almost every new car that is manufactured has the capability to travel over one hundred miles per hour. **Now comes the bullshit:** Almost nowhere in existence can the average person legally or safely do so. Here's my thing: if an individual is going to be able to possess a certain amount of power but not be able to use that power to its full potential, won't that person be the least bit tempted – and not only that, wouldn't that be a complete waste of resources and time? Take a Lamborghini for example. These cars have the capability to exceed not one but two hundred miles per hour (That's about a thousand dollars per mph) Now ask yourself, what possible reason could there be for needing to go that fast? I have been in a car with a fool who was driving one hundred and twenty miles per hour and while I was silently cursing this fool and at the same time praying that I would walk away with my life, I had the opportunity to look out at the cars on the NJ Turnpike that were doing what seemed to be the speed limit or close to it. These cars literally looked like they were going in slow motion. With that being said, can anybody with half an ounce of common sense explain to me the need to be able to go two hundred miles a fucking hour? In the streets of New York, it cannot be done. In almost every city I have traveled to, it cannot be done. The only feasible place it could be done other than the Autobahn in Germany is on a race track and then the cars would have to be equipped for racing, plus the drivers would have to wear helmets, which I believe would prove futile because if a person were to drive that fast and involve himself in an accident, there is no conceivable way he would live. If by some really ginormous stretch of the imagination or Divine intervention, this person did not die, what purpose other than giving the hospital aides who change the bed sheets something to do, could he serve? Now let's just say again that a person could control a vehicle going that fast and he weren't racing, the question still remains, why? Here's a kind of novel idea; why not make the limit on the speedometer equal to the limit on the posted signs? It would really cut down on speeding – don't ya think? I know there are different speed limits in different parts of the country but absolutely nowhere have I seen one, which states that's it's allowable to drive one hundred and sixty miles per hour. As stated before, what I think car manufactures should do is take the highest speed limit they can find (within reason of course) and set that as the standard for all vehicles that are not intended specifically for racing. I believe this car thing has a lot in common with this gun thing everybody's so embroiled in controversy about. Personally, I like guns, always have. I like to shoot them. I like to collect them. I also believe in everybody's right to bear arms. With that being said, remember that this is America and as unfortunate as it is to say, no matter where you go, you more than likely will encounter at least one asshole who will want to run up in your home and try to take your hard earned assets or try to hurt a member of your family or who will just want to kill you because you look like somebody they do not like. For reasons such as these and more I think it is okay to protect one's self with any ole garden variety (licensed of course) 9mm handgun they may have lying around the house. What I do not believe it is okay to do is own, possess, manufacture or any way be associated with a weapon that has the capability to fire over one hundred rounds in a matter of seconds. This is wrong. This is appalling. This is fucking crazy. I mean where's the logic? I have always considered myself a reasonable man but where in the realm of reasonableness can any reasonable person see that there is a market for understanding the logic behind this? An automatic weapon or street sweeper, as they are commonly called, in my opinion is for use in the military or by law enforcement personnel only. I say this because I have been in the military and have handled my share of automatic weapons but not only that, I have, as I believe most in the military have, been trained in the proper way to handle these weapons safely. I know that there are a lot of people on the street who have automatic weapons and I am undoubtedly certain that all of these people that possess these weapons have not been trained in the safest manner of operation possible. (This being due to the so called stringent gun control laws which are supposed to stop the flow of illegal weapons into our country and cities.) In other words, it's easier to gun a gun than it is to safely and properly learn how to use it. Think about something; guns are not perfect. Sometimes they jam and will not fire. Sometimes they get stuck in the firing position (which means they will continue firing until the weapon is empty). Now either of these things can happen because of a failure by the company to diagnose a potential problem later on or because of the owner not knowing that a gun must be regularly cleaned for safe and proper operation. What if some knucklehead gets hold of an automatic weapon which has an unbelievably ridiculous amount of fire power which has not been cleaned for maybe a couple of years? And what if this knucklehead decides to shoot someone he doesn't like and the gun keeps firing after he lets go of the trigger? And still, what if he gets scared and drops the gun and it begins shooting any and everything in its path? Somebody more than likely will become an unintentional victim. I remember in the military, having to clean my weapon after each usage. I remember also having to be able to completely disassemble my weapon and reassemble it blindfolded. This, I believe was to ensure that I knew how to not only operate it but repair it in low light conditions if need be. My question is – does the average Joe Knucklehead who gets an automatic weapon know how to do this? Would the average Joe Knucklehead even care? I think not. In my opinion, there should be no controversy at all. Guns which possess so much firepower, just like cars which can go almost and above two hundred miles per hour have no place in a reasonable society. Everybody in this world does not always think logically. Sometimes people think and buy on impulse. The main definition of impulse shopping is buying something you want then justifying it later. What will happen if you or anybody else buys a car and the pedal gets stuck while you are going over one hundred miles per hour or as stated above the gun somebody uses gets stuck while firing? People will get hurt. We're not only talking about the jackasses who didn't think before using these items of mass destruction but we're talking about completely innocent ones too.

On Dating

Many eons ago, there existed a practice of committed friendship called dating. It entailed a young man and a young woman being romantically linked without interference from any other party. This usually meant that the couple was going steady. It did not mean that either party was free to go and stick or get stuck by any and everybody and then come back home to the person they were dating. Now the term dating has taken on a whole new meaning. The new updated interpretation of dating is a couple will or will not have sex and be romantically linked to one another but they will each share the freedom to 'date' whoever else they desire, unless of course they throw in that much desired but much more misinterpreted word; exclusive. **Now here comes the bullshit:** Exclusive is little more than a word. It is little more than the belief that the person you have promised your heart to will do the same. This is kinda like the whole marriage fallacy. The only difference with that is there's a magical ring, which is supposed to keep the parties involved exclusive. Ha. Marriage is supposed to be the epitome of exclusivity when it comes to dating. It is supposed to be dating but with only one person for life. Again, ha. Dating nowadays legitimizes being a hoe and it does so under the pretense of weeding out the bad apples in search of Mr. or Mrs. Right. Dating has gone from dealing with one person, with the ultimate goal of finding out everything or as much as you can about this person to see if that person is actually marriage material or if not marriage material then at least a long term prospect – all the way to what these silly assed reality shows have gently misconstrued it into being - and that is little more than a fuck fest. Dating used to be the first step in 'I'm interested in this particular person and I want to eventually have a permanent or at least long term relationship with this particular person' but as of late and much thanks to the media and society at large, when a person is dating, they are doing what's known as 'exploring' their options. In other words, they are allowed to have as many sexual or non sexual partners as possible. They are almost never exclusive because the term exclusive is now interpreted to mean a relationship – and this is in direct contrast to the original meaning of dating.

The thing about dating that many people do not understand is that when you date someone, you are not only dating him or her, you are dating that person's interpretation of what a relationship is. This is not gender based but many times gender does play a major part in how many people see their roles in dating and relationships. The problem with these roles, whichever they may be, is that they are almost never the same as the person a person is interested in. Many women, not all but many like to think that when they are dating exclusively, they are in a relationship which will eventually become a marriage or if not a marriage, then a lifelong relationship. And this is because many of these women do not set guidelines or boundaries on what their dating is to entail or become. Some of these women have this belief that the men they are interested in will automatically propose marriage because he is in a committed relationship already and proposing marriage is not much of a jump from that. But see here comes the hypocrisy, deception or whatever you wanna call it; many guys are not really focused on longevity when it comes to dating. Many of them are focused on good times and as long as they exist, the <u>potential</u> for longevity is there. Some women think like 'well he always makes me happy so I will try and keep him around for the long term and he hasn't said anything to the contrary, meaning he hasn't said that he <u>doesn't</u> want to stay around, so he must <u>want</u> to be around for the long term.' Some guys think like 'well she makes me happy, so I'm gonna stay around as long as she continues to do so.' Dating regrettably has a lot in common with marriage and the belief of the committed relationship. I say this because there has to be ongoing communication in these types of unions for them to exist and prevail. What dating regrettably has in common with these other unions is that the communication is often flawed – meaning it is only in place to achieve a certain goal. Instead of the communication being about any and everything, the way I believe it should be, it is mainly about what will provide the immediate gratification. People will always have different interpretations on everything in life but when people don't come to some sort of agreement on things as important as relationships, when they are in the beginning stages as with dating or whether they are in the middle or ending stages, those relationships will become fake. Many people start off with agendas, which are not completely honest and they do so because they want to obtain something that they otherwise would not have been able to obtain had they told the complete truth. This is not new or unheard of but it does lead to problems down the line because if the relationship's foundation is not built on honesty, then the relationship is guaranteed to fail. When people are not honest about what it is they want from the dating, whether it is some sex, some companionship or an all out relationship that will eventually lead to marriage, the relationship will, let me say it again, the relationship will definitely fail.

On This Whole Sex Thing

Sex is one of the greatest feelings in the world. **Now here comes the bullshit:** Sex is one of the most manipulated and stipulated things in this world. The reason behind why the act of sexual intercourse is done is one, which is often misunderstood. It is misunderstood because people have hidden agendas, hidden desires and even hidden perversions, which they cleverly conceal until after the sex is had or until after the relationship is initiated. Aside from the above, people will almost never relay to the other person what sex means to them. They will most often agree with whatever it is that sex means to the other just to make the relationship go easier or to get what it is they want from the relationship. Some people will say that sex is just a physical act and as such, once the act is over, so will be the feelings, which were shared during the sex act. But we all know this is bullshit. If this weren't bullshit, there wouldn't be things such as stalkers. There wouldn't be things such as murder suicides over infidelity. And there sure as hell wouldn't be anyone asking that stupid ass question, do you love the person that you cheated on me with? Some people will say that the act of sex is a sacred one, which should only be attempted in the pursuit or procreation of life. And there will be a great percentage of the population, which will agree with this statement just so that they can engage in the sex act. But we all know that this is bullshit too. If this weren't bullshit, people would only be indulging or engaging in sex acts once every nine or so months. The thing that most people do not want to admit is that when it comes to sex, there are always feelings involved.

Another thing about sex is that it can no longer be just enjoyed. It seems that now it has deteriorated to the point of where it has to be either manipulated or bought. I mean think about it – what would happen if the average guy walked up to the average woman, whom he did not know and said 'hey my name is so & so, let's have sex.' Chances are he would get the shit slapped out of him and this is again thanks to society. Society has placed such a stigma on most things that if there is any type of deviance from the accepted pattern of what society expects, then it's wrong. Continuing with the above example but on the opposite end of the gender spectrum, let's say a woman walked up to the average man on the street and said 'hey, my name is so & so, let's have sex' after the initial thought of 'yippie' and 'hell yea!' the guy would probably begin to think, 'wait a minute, something's wrong here. Is she crazy? Does she have an STD that she wants to spread to anybody who will take it? Am I on one of those hidden camera shows? And the reason why this guy would think these things is because even though this is probably what he has been dreaming, hoping and wishing that some woman would come and say to him, it is not normal. Nowadays, the expectation is that sex has to come with some kind of hesitation or headache. It's not always a bad thing because immediately jumping into bed with the first person you see may have disastrous results. Nowadays people fall into one of two categories: they either have to run some sort of game to get the one they are involved in a relationship with or interested in to have sex with them or they have to make the sex act a business dealing. The problem with this is that even though most will agree its true, most will not accept it. Let's take women for example; even though the vast majority of them are fully aware that men desire to, at some point in the relationship, get into their drawers, they will act like they are in control of the situation all along or they will act like they don't know what the man is after. They will use every delay tactic they can think of. They will play whatever type of game they can fathom. They will make a man do anything to prove his worthiness. Now take men for example; men play games when it comes to the pursuit of sex as well. They lie to make it seem that they are not as interested as they actually are. They manipulate their feelings to resemble what it is the women want in regard to sex, so that they can have sex or they just pay for it. The problem between the sexes is that people think sex is something more than what it actually is. When it comes to sex in relationships, the bottom line is that it is done for basically two reasons. The first is for fun. The second is for children. People cause detriment to themselves by adding things to the sex act, which shouldn't be added. People add unspoken stipulations such as, if I have sex with this person, then this person will love me. People say I know I said that sex was only going to be a physical act but I want a relationship and after we have sex, that is what it will be whether they want it or not. People say I'm gonna have a baby and this will cause the physical act to become a lifelong relationship and not only that – the person will learn to love me because of the baby. These things bring about detriment to the relationship because for one, they are unspoken. For two, they are not always what the other person in the relationship wants. Sex is simple – either a person wants to have babies when they do it or they don't. How people manipulate the sex act is by lying, deceiving and perpetrating any and every type of trickery to make the other believe that there are other reasons why the sex act is being perpetrated.

On Credit Scores

Credit scores are supposed to gauge an individual's credit worthiness. In other words, these magical numbers when combined, calculated or averaged will enable an individual to easily buy a car or a home or some other big ticket item. **Now here comes the bullshit:** These numbers are not the same for everybody. Apparently, someone in charge has come to the belief and understanding that the higher a person's credit score is, the better suited that person is to receive a loan or actual credit for an actual big ticket purchase. I believe that this is bullshit because a person's past is almost never an accurate indicator of that person's future. Sometimes people pay their bills on time because they have a good job as well as someone around to make sure that the bills are paid on time. This could be a case where the husband is the breadwinner but he is absolutely inept when it comes to budgeting or keeping track of what needs to be paid. They wife may be unemployed but an ace at recordkeeping. The husband can get paid every week or two and give his entire paycheck to the wife to let her disburse it as she sees fit. Now what does this do? This makes the husband seem as if he has the best credit worthiness in the world. Again this is bullshit because what if the husband in this scenario just happens to lose his good paying job or lose his ace recordkeeping wife. That A-1 credit rating will be shot! But this is the nonsense that many of these credit agencies go by. They figure that what has been done in the past is what will be done in the future. And this does not only apply to the positive side of the credit game but also the negative. If a person has had a few bankruptcies or unpaid loans or even foreclosures, the general consensus will be that that person is and will continue to be a bad credit risk. What these credit companies should know is that just as a marriage could be the cause of a great credit rating, it could be the cause of an adverse one as well. Sometimes the breadwinner has an abundance of good credit but the significant other has a habit of impulse buying and not only that but also a habit of forgetting to pay bills when they are due. If this system of bestowing credit to those who have had a favorable credit history was applied to other things in life, for instance the stock market, investors would never lose money. All they would do is follow the pattern of history. If a stock was doing well, then it would continue to do well. If a person bought a used car from ABC dealership and that car performed perfectly, then it would make sense to reason that every other future car purchased from ABC dealership would fare just as well. If this method was applied to relationships, every subsequent year of togetherness would be just as wonderful as the first just because of how wonderful the first year was. Am I the only one who sees a pattern of bullshit here? Credit scores are what people unnecessarily fear because credit companies unfairly use them to make the life of regular people hell. A credit score is an asinine way of determining what type of person an individual is just by when that person pays his bills.

I have noticed that regarding employment some companies now find it necessary to check a prospective employee's credit history before that individual is offered a position. My question is what kind of bullshit is that? Why do companies need to check your credit score for you to get a job? Is it that if you have a positive history of paying your bills on time, you will automatically make a good employee? I will be the first to admit that my credit is beyond fucked up but that does not make me a bad worker. This, in my opinion is little more than another attempt by the powers that be to control more of your everyday life. Why does anybody need to know how good or bad anybody's credit is? Unless of course they want to manipulate it or give you more of it. I seriously doubt that an individual needs to apply for a job to receive a credit increase. This practice that more and more companies are starting to indulge in makes it seem like an individual has to be perfect in every aspect of his or her life before he or she can get a job. Lying on resumes is not enough anymore. Now an individual has to be able to erase bad credit from public record to be able to get a job. That's some real bullshit, ain't it?

On Police

There will never be a completely effective system of power as long as it is man made. And this is because everything man made is susceptible to corruption. From my experience, police do not follow a textbook system for upholding the law. They follow a system of whatever works. My proof of this is having 'interacted' with a couple of officers on more than one occasion for the same infraction. The first time I was let off with a warning. The second time, well let's just say it was not as favorable as the first. The police are supposed to be abiding by what they are taught in the academy, as well as the penal code, among other things but from my experience and the experiences of many others, quite often the police will do whatever they deem 'necessary' to get the job done. I guess this is where the term 'necessary force' emanates. I do understand that in certain situations, a little more force than sternly talking to a suspected criminal is necessary to apprehend said criminal but who's to say when enough is enough? The problem with people is the fact that everybody is different on so many levels. **Now here comes the bullshit.** Because police are given guns, quite often they let those guns overtake their common sense. This means that because they feel their lives are in danger or because they have personal grudges against certain individuals or races they can unload twenty, thirty or fifty plus bullets on a single individual. And here's the real bullshit; sometimes these motherfuckers actually get away with it! I am not a cop nor can I imagine what these police officers have to endure on a daily basis but this type of job is not one where a loss of control can be expected or tolerated. Trust me, living in New York, especially the city, will make you really want to hurt some people but when you are entrusted with protecting these individuals, such as police are, you have to think before you act – not act in a questionable or unacceptable manner, then get your friends to help you cover it up. Now I do understand that there will always be differences in how people are taught, how people learn, how people react and respond to situations but there has to be some universal protocol and accountability for those that choose to wear the uniform. There are going to be those individuals, when relating to certain situations, who will over react and there will be those individuals who will under react as well. What if there is a situation, which calls for a certain type of response and the dispatched or responding officers over react and someone loses his or her life because of it or what if a situation arises where an officer under reacts and again, a life is lost? Will the general public give these officers leeway by saying it's okay, mistakes happen? Will there be worldwide acceptance of the fact that not everybody will respond to every situation in the exact same manner? Or will there be public outrage and outcry every time something does not go according to plan? What is really bullshit about the police are not so much the actions of some of their officers but the perceptions of their actual job description to society at large. Just like they have different methods of doing their jobs, many people in this world have different interpretations on what it is law enforcement can do, what they can't do and what it is they are supposed to do. Some people think that when a person is a cop, that person is above God. Some police personnel think that too. Now from my understanding, there are certain factions who are supposed to keep tabs on the corruption and misappropriation of funds and things like that but my question is 'who is going to keep tabs on the tab keepers?' As I said before, everybody's human and as such; everybody is susceptible to temptation and failure. The fact that some people in law enforcement think they can't be touched is bullshit. The fact that people outside of law enforcement think that those in law enforcement are above the law is bullshit even more.

On another bullshit note, I have to ask, why it that certain crimes are only crimes for certain people? I have seen police officers (I won't mention from which precinct) allow a woman to slap the shit out of a man but apprehend the man when he does the same. Okay granted, a lot of men are stronger than a lot of women but does that excuse the fact that an assault occurred by both parties? I have witnessed a male police officer excuse a minor traffic infraction committed by a pretty woman but give me a ticket. My thing is; why can't you so called fair and honest officers of the law treat everybody the same? That means if a man and woman both break the law, then both the man and woman should face the same penalty. Not one given a warning because she has big tits and a pretty smile or because she gives the officer the impression that she will give him some ass on a later date. If police actually realized that sometimes women carry weapons and drugs for their significant others, they might actually stop everybody that walks into the projects instead of only minority

28

males. Now by no means am I saying that I want police to stop everybody that decides to venture into the projects on any given day – I am just saying that this profiling shit really needs to take a sharp turn in the downward direction. For once in my life, I would like nothing more than to travel into a predominately white neighborhood and witness three or four black men ride up to the first – matter of fact ride up to every white male they see walking (who may or may not fit that imaginary profile) and pat him down, go through his pockets and ask him what he's doing, where's he's going and if he's had anything to drink that particular day as I have had done on numerous occasions. Would there be public outcry or would these white folks just accept it the same way many minority folks seem to do? I'll tell you what would happen; these white folks would lose their fucking minds. But here's the bullshit: for some reason or other, law enforcement personnel seem to honestly believe that if you happen to live in a certain area, whether you work or not, if there is a certain amount of pigmentation in your skin, you are automatically deemed a criminal. Ain't that some shit? Then some cops actually wonder why some people have such a bad feeling about police in general. I know some people are bad but everybody isn't. Why don't you cops wait until somebody does something bad and arrest them (Like I believe it's supposed to be) instead of arresting or harassing any garden variety individual who just happens to stroll on by and who happens to be of a particular race. I am aware also that there are some individuals who have multiple murder or kidnapping and rape warrants and need to be off the streets but is the only effective way you have of enacting this policy the one of stopping everybody who again happens to be of a particular race? What happened to more diligent police work? Police do not have a history for helping people stay out of jail. Police don't say 'this will help you stay out of jail' they say 'let's wait until he does something stupid or appears to do something stupid, so we can lock his ass up.' And then they wonder why so many people are in jail. Here's a novel idea – if people have warrants for things considered 'not so serious' instead of sending the warrant squad to their homes at six in the damn morning, why not create a permanent amnesty program where hard working people who may have made a mistake or two or who may have just gotten caught up in some bullshit police sting have the chance to take care of those warrants by giving them more time to pay or even creating a pay a little each week program? Funny how the powers that be will allow an individual to cement himself into the inescapable credit trap by letting said individual pay a little bit of a ginormous purchase price of some unnecessary impulse item each week but will not let that individual do the same to help him prevent himself from a negative reputation when it comes to his criminal record. Something as simple as this would keep people out of jail and subsequently prevent them from losing their jobs and possibly homes as well as the ability to get other jobs. But no – law enforcement does not want to do this. They want to lock up the bad guy and throw away the key. Again I ask, is there any wonder why people dislike cops? I remember when I was young and the police used to come to our school on career day and tell us about how wonderful it was to be a cop and help protect people from the bad guys and all that crap that our young and innocent minds used to soak up like sponges. Now a person would be hard pressed to find to find someone over the age of sixteen who would really consider that profession. I mean don't get me wrong, I do respect the job cops do, rather are supposed to do but I do not respect the few who make it bad for the many. I do not respect those officers driving through my neighborhood at night with deeply tinted windows and license plates which are bent in such a way so that you cannot read them and therefore report them after they commit their illegal stop and search and assault tactics. That's some real bullshit there. Some of these cops and I use that term loosely, won't even go through the trouble of bending the license plate. They will just remove that shit and drive around like the untouchable motherfuckers they want the average individual to think they are. There was a time when cops would be the ones to turn to when the criminals made a peaceful existence too much to fathom. Now it's hard for a person to tell who to fear, the criminals or the police. Now some people can't tell the difference. Here's an example: I have seen with my own eyes, a policeman jump out of a van, take his radio and strike a black male on the top of his head because he was selling cigarettes and decided to run when the police van came by. One of the officers got out and after this individual stopped, struck him to get him to fall down. I ask you; is this proper police protocol or is this some turn of the century, slavery inspired bullshit? What is so hard with requesting the man get down on his knees or belly or whatever and then hand cuffing him and then doing whatever it is police are supposed to do? Why do cops or some cops have to commit violent acts or instill fear first, then ask questions later? It's because some of you motherfuckers are full of shit. Yes I know this is harsh language and it is not directed against any one precinct but seriously now, is this the only way you can do your jobs? I have been on the receiving end of brutality by the cops also and I do apologize if my tirade offends some of the good cops out there but the shit that some of you motherfuckers perpetrate is just wrong. I also saw eight, count 'em 8 police officers chasing a young man on a motorcycle. The man stopped his bike on 166th street and Ogden Avenue in the Bronx. I know this because I and several other people were waiting for a bus at that time directly across the street. Now I do not know what the previous circumstances were surrounding this man's pursuit but he stopped his bike and put his hands up. The police officers, rather the first responding police officers grabbed the man and threw him to the ground and kicked him repeatedly before he was handcuffed. I ask you why? From my observation, interpretation and experience, when an individual has his hands up, that individual is not really asking for trouble but then again maybe the police have some new understanding where up raised arms resemble a threatening motion. Whatever happened to innocent until PROVEN guilty? I'll tell you what happened to it; it never existed. All innocent until proven guilty ever meant was we, the powers that be, will let you think that we believe you're innocent until we show you and everybody else without a shadow of a doubt that you were guilty all along. If the idea behind the innocent until proven guilty charade were anything more than just a way to pacify honest, law abiding people into believing that justice and fairness and equality and all that good shit really existed, then the criminal justice system of this country would probably not be looked upon as a joke. Think about something: if an individual was seriously innocent until proven guilty, would that individual be arrested in the first place? I mean is it commonplace for the members of law enforcement to go around arresting innocent people and then holding them until their actual guilt is proven? That would be a travesty of justice. But then again, that's just my opinion. I honestly believe that police tactics really need to be re evaluated – no fuck that, they need to be changed. You can be effective without being feared. Police, it's not too late for you to be respected – instead of hated…assholes.

Here's one more instance before I close this section of police and their bullshit – In Seattle, an officer of the law was video taped punching a female in the face. Did it matter that he was white and she was black? Did it matter that he was a larger male and she was a smaller woman? Did it matter that he could have just (given his size) handcuffed her and placed her in the back seat? No, these things didn't matter at all because apparently all that mattered was the fact that he was the officer and she was somebody who either threatened his authority or threatened his manhood. In my opinion, I believe that there was no feasible or conceivable reason for this action unless the officer felt that his safety was in jeopardy. If the average person were to look at the video on you tube, (cop punches girl) it would be a pretty safe bet that they would not find anything even remotely resembling a threatening situation, which would cause the officer to react in such a manner. Okay granted, the lady did push the officer but from my understanding the officer did not suffer any injury and it appears that the officer responded because he was angry. This appears to me like another loss of control that many in the police departments around this country are famous for. Now I'm sure that somebody in the police department or some waste of semen will find some merit in the officer's actions. They will probably say something to the effect of the officer was defending himself and I'm all for self defense but maybe if the woman were twice his size and had him pinned underneath the front wheel of his patrol car or maybe if the individual was a male the same size as the officer in question, I could possibly understand but this woman was smaller than he was. There is no understanding there. Growing up in my community, one of the basic unwritten rules was 'boys do not hit girls, boys walk away.' I guess this officer was never taught that or maybe he was taught that everybody who is not a cop is a criminal or maybe, just maybe he doesn't like girls. I'm just saying. Here's a question; what ever happened to calling for backup? Would the responding cops have laughed at him because he was not able to handle a couple of females? I understand the idea behind reasonable force and all but when does it become reasonable to punch a woman in the face – especially when she didn't punch first? I do not know what cops are taught is an effective measure of force but wouldn't reasonable force be the same force used upon them? Would there be any outcry if the officer in question had pushed her the way she pushed him? I think not. Punching someone is an act of violence. Punching someone who is smaller than you is an act of showing dominance. Some may even say an act of cowardice. A person really has to ask himself; how far away is this officer's actions from pulling out his gun?

Okay I know I said I was trying to close the chapter on police and their bullshit but every time I try, some new bullshit pops up which I feel I absolutely must share. At the time of this book's printing, there is an ongoing situation, which involves the esteemed NY police department. This situation revolves around the ticket fixing scandal, which several cops have been caught up in. Now I am not the first to realize or speculate that there is or may be some kind of corruption going on in the police department. I do not know how widespread it is but there is corruption. And the main reason corruption exists is because the department is run by humans. Humans are the most corruptible resource on earth, so I am not pointing the finger at any one precinct or any one individual but here comes the bullshit: many of the members of the police department I guess in a show of solidarity, are protesting the arrests of the officers who were caught. These people are saying that one of the reasons why the law was broken was due to common courtesy. Now I'm confused; according to the protesting officers, it's okay to break the law to do someone a favor but it's not okay to break the law to do a favor for someone if you are not a member of law enforcement. Is that about right? I know about the ignorance of the law is no excuse thing but what about the ignorance of the law that favoritism overlooks? This is one of the reasons that many in the police department are not completely loved or respected. The law does not apply to everybody. It only applies to the other guy. This means that if I don't know you, then the law applies. This means that if I don't like you, then the law applies. This means that if I do know you and I like you, we can bend the law somewhat – as a courtesy. That's some bullshit. If courtesy was actually a reason to break the law or bend it, however you wanna classify it, then the courtesy excuse would apply to everybody – men, women, Black, White, Puerto Rican, Jew, Gentile, assemblyman, judge or security guard. But we know that will never happen and why, because fairness is not cast in stone. It is most often up to the discretion of an individual. If they feel like doing their job, they will. If they don't, they won't. Now don't get me wrong; I do believe that once in a while a person is entitled to a break – as in letting said person off with a warning. But these laws which are not cast in stone or that are able to be overlooked should be made known publicly and not enforced only when an officer feels like enforcing them. If a person gets a parking ticket, they should either be made to pay it or they should get their car towed as I have had mine on several occasions. I had a friend who used a weapon to protect somebody on the train who was being hassled by some thugs. It did not matter that my friend didn't know the individual he was protecting. He just believed it was the right thing to do. It did not matter to the police either, because he was arrested and sentenced to a couple of years for trying to do what he thought was right. I was always led to believe that courtesy could best be described as helping somebody. My friend attempted to do something courteous and was penalized for it. Where was the courtesy on the part of the police department in that case? Why didn't they say 'well you did prevent somebody from getting robbed or assaulted by using your weapon and since nobody really got hurt, I guess we could just make this charge go away…' but it didn't happen like that – and the main reason why I believe it didn't is because this system of justice that we have is on some real bullshit – but that's just my opinion. I tell you one thing though; I am willing to bet that everybody who was on that train that night as well as everybody reading this who has ever been in a situation where they needed help and couldn't find any would have loved to have had my friend and his weapon there to stand up for them and provide a courtesy – but then again, maybe I'm just rambling.

I remember one time way back when I needed to take the train but did not have enough money to afford the train fare. At that time I did not have a bank account to supplement my existence either. So what did I do? I did what any other individual who had no money and no immediate resources would do. I hopped over the turnstile. Just my luck there happened to be a NYC transit cop sitting there waiting to penalize me for doing so. Was I wrong for breaking the law? Yes. Was he wrong for doing his job? No. But could he have been courteous and let me go with a warning? Hell yea.

But did he? Hell no. Asshole. Point I am trying to make is that everything can be overlooked. With that being said, my question is why is it that these things, which can be overlooked are only overlooked by certain individuals and only for certain individuals? Crimes should be crimes for everybody or courtesies should be courtesies for all. Anything else is bullshit.

On Parking Violations

Now I will be the first to admit that there must be some kind of order and control in today's world for it to exist properly and or peacefully but some things, rather some laws are just taking this theory completely out of hand. I try to respect every honest job because I honestly believe that each job has a purpose for the betterment of society. However it seems that these cops, rather these individuals who work for the Parking Violations Bureau seem like they have a perpetual ax to grind with everybody they do not know. I have witnessed traffic cops hovering around a meter, which had about a minute of time left on it and wait until that minute actually ran out to start writing a ticket. That's some real bullshit there. Would it have killed to walk down the block and then make that u turn back to the original location to just give the poor sap who owns the car maybe just an extra minute or two to move his car and avoid getting that $115 ticket? A lot of people who have cars can barely afford the car notes and insurance but to add a ticket and an unnecessary one at that? Real bullshit. I have had a boot put on my car because I parked inside of a McDonald's parking lot and did not immediately go inside of the restaurant. My thing is how did these cocksuckers know that I wasn't going to go into the restaurant later? I mean I do understand the need for parking for customers but this was early in the day and there were about twenty other free spaces. I think the boot people just wanted to be dicks! I wasn't away from the car for literally five minutes! What's up with that? That's bullshit right there. Now there are some things being ticketed for I can completely understand, for instance – parking in front of a hydrant. Reason being; what if there is a fire and the fire trucks can't see or immediately gain access to the hydrant because your car is blocking it? I can even see the justification of giving somebody a ticket because they are double parked on a small street, making passing by other cars either impossible or dangerous. But how can you reasonably justify giving someone a ticket for parking at a no standing anytime spot when there is no sign indicating that there is no standing or no parking allowed? Now granted the pole which the sign was on was destroyed and most of the people who lived on the block that the sign was on knew what the sign was for but what about the people who did not live in the neighborhood and had just happened to be driving by? I witnessed this firsthand and asked the traffic agent about why he was giving a ticket when the sign was destroyed and he responded 'It's still a No Standing Zone.' I asked well how is somebody supposed to know that and he said they can dispute it in court. That's some real bullshit there.

Another thing I consider to be an unbelievably large amount of bullshit is the if you don't pay a ticket in a certain amount of time, they get to charge you more money. Like that's really gonna entice a person to make payment. Common sense dictates that if an individual does not have enough money to pay the original fine, how in the hell will that individual be able to pay that fine plus some? If payment is really desired and this whole ticket thing is not just some clever scam to get money to the city, then why not lessen the amount of the fine and give the poor sap who got the ticket a fair chance to pay? I'm pretty sure the powers that be will never do that. They will just keep increasing the amount that is due probably in the hopes that the poor sap who got the ticket will get a better job and be able to afford the ticket price plus the surcharges and related fees – but if by chance he doesn't get a better job, then there will be a warrant put out for his arrest which will more than likely cost him his job and then eventually his license because he has no job now to pay the tickets anyway.

About a couple of months before this book actually went to print, there was quite a big controversy going on which revolved around certain members of law enforcement giving breaks or as they put it 'courtesies' to certain other people when it comes to the payment of traffic tickets. This courtesy basically allows certain individuals to get away with not paying these tickets because the tickets are made to disappear. I am all for courtesy but only when it applies to everybody. When courtesy applies to certain individuals, it is called favoritism. And favoritism is bullshit. A definition of favoritism is preferential treatment to one at the expense of another. Now I will admit that I do not know the entire story behind why the preferential treatment was given to certain individuals - meaning whether it was requested by superiors or just a judgment call on the part of the officers who chose to undertake that action but my thing is if a courtesy can't be shown for everybody, at least once, then it should not be shown for anybody. I'm just saying.

On Relationships

In case you haven't noticed by now, everything I write is, not speculation but what I believe to be (from personal experience and research) honest to God truth. This section is no exception. In my opinion, relationships are bad. The idea of relationships however, is quite the opposite. I'm guessing that most of the single people in this world would like to believe that a relationship is almost always happy and always progressing toward some new and uncharted level. I'm guessing also that many of them would like to believe that their chosen soul mate would always be in their corner, to hold them down so to speak. Many of these people would feel that there would be no such thing as secrets, possible infidelity or the happy relationship ever losing its jubilation. This is a partial explanation of the idea behind many relationships in this world. Note: the idea of a relationship is much more pacifying and desired than that of an actual relationship because actual relationships cause pain, sometimes severe pain. I believe relationships are bad because of the following: many people in relationships or those contemplating relationships have grown to expect a certain type of behavior or protocol regarding how their relationships are going to turn out. These people, men and women, feel that they are going to have partners who will do this for them, partners who will do that for them, partners who will respond to their every beck and call. They feel that the relationship will not go sour unless there is some negative outside intervention. They feel that their partners will be perfect in every way and life as they know it will be wonderful. **Now here comes the bullshit:** This is the complacency cottage many people in relationships reside in. This is the result of unrealistic expectations. Many people live under this façade because they feel that the amount of happiness that is present in the beginning of the relationship will continue throughout the relationship – even if it takes a break here and there. These people feel that the initial magic will just resurface whenever necessary and rectify any problems within the union. This is bullshit because everybody knows that a relationship is about, if nothing else, honesty and communication. It is not about wishing and hoping. What everybody does not always know is how to get these things across to their significant others. Many people in relationships feel that things like honesty and communication are a relationship birthright. In other words, some feel that no matter what, once a couple becomes a couple, honesty will initiate and continue without any effort from the parties involved. This is more bullshit. People will only use honesty when it's convenient. A prime example of this is how when people get caught cheating on their significant others they will avoid admitting the truth at any and all costs but when they are the ones who catch their significant others cheating, they expect, rather demand truth and honesty. See the hypocrisy? Couples have and have always had different interpretations of what relationships actually entail. Couples often have different agendas when it comes to the longevity of their particular relationship but they will alter those agendas so that they do not upset the agenda of the other. Proof of this is how many women want to get married before they even start dating. The thing which is deceptive and disheartening about this is the fact that many of these women will never tell the individual they are involved with their agenda until they are well into the relationship or until they are pregnant with this individual's child. More proof of this is how men are historically known for 'shopping around' three, four and five times as much as women do before they choose someone to commit to. Spare me all that crap about the double standard and such, relationships are about agendas. And just like the women, some of these men will never tell the women they are pursuing that they may just be one of many or one for the time being. Women are guilty of this too. I have seen and heard on more occasions than I can even bother to count at the present time, potty mouthed women who expel verbal excrement at more than twice the rate and vulgarity than that of men. I have been on a semi packed train where three well dressed women who had just noticed a good looking man began to talk about how they wanted to fuck the shit out of this man. There was no discretion. There was no 'I shouldn't talk this way because I'm a woman. There was just straight up locker room language. Now my thing is an individual can have desires, no matter how vile or disgusting but not divulging those vile and disgusting desires to the one you have them about is what contributes to failed relationships. This fits right into the much dreaded by most men and those people who are usually deceptive and deceitful, communication. Now everybody in a relationship, those contemplating a relationship and those who ever even heard of a relationship know that communication is a necessity for a

40

relationships' existence and continuance. However, as with the honesty issue stated above, many people are under the impression or illusion that communication will come with the relationship just as batteries will come with an electronic toy. But just like the electronic toy on Christmas morning, many people don't figure out batteries are necessary until after the fact. What people do in so many relationship situations is avoid talking in the hopes that if they don't venture into dangerous or sensitive territory, that way there will never be any reason to argue or become upset. This is a highly favored method of prolonging the inevitable. When people do not talk about things, which are causing them displeasure, these things will never go away. If they do go away, eventually they will resurface and cause detriment to their peace of mind. Let me see if I can simplify the deterioration process: Boy meets girl. Boy likes girl. Boy and girl become a couple. Boy does not tell girl that he is only interested in her for sexual gratification. Girl does not tell boy that she desires and expects marriage in a certain amount of time. (Deception by omission leads to the erosion of honesty.) Some people think that a person can only be deceptive by lying. Sometimes a person can be deceptive by not saying anything. The relationship continues on a slow to fast downward spiral because there is no communication on what was truly desired in the relationship. In other words the relationship was a fake because the true agendas were never revealed. This is what makes trusting someone so damned hard. People always say I want the truth. I need the truth. I deal in nothing but the truth. What happens when these people start to realize that many, maybe not most but many of the people in this world whom they are interested in will not share in their quest for complete honesty? Will they have the resilience and strength to push them aside while they continue their search for complete honesty? I think not. You see everybody in this world knows or should know that complete honesty causes pain. People say that they want to be able to trust the person they involve themselves with but how can they – especially when a person can never tell if the one they are involved with is being honest or deceptive?

If a person were to really examine it, he would find that the trust issue is bullshit by itself – if it weren't then couples could be in a relationship and live apart couldn't they? Not theoretically but actually. People want their relationships to follow historical perspectives and not their own. Many people want to keep their own places when they either get married or deeply committed but 'society' says that that desire is taboo. 'Society' says if you can't give up a small part of your independence (as what some people call having their own place) then you are not truly in love. Some people just feel that other relationships have to dictate their relationships. The other relationships could be that of a mother and father or that of friends but here's the thing; some people have gotten so far away from the belief that they can actually be different from the crowd that they are even scared to try. Ask yourself honestly – could you allow the man or woman you are involved with whether that involvement be a marriage or boyfriend and girlfriend type of union to live by themselves while you live by yourself? Most people will not even consider this question because they have these preset agendas in their minds that many times they don't even know they have. And because people don't speak about these things before hand, they are setting the stage for failure. I mean honestly, if there were real trust in a relationship and I don't mean satisfactory trust which says that as long as my partner doesn't give me reason to not trust him then I do but real and complete trust, would it really matter if a couple lived apart? What really is the difference between 'I have my place and a copy of your key' and you have your place and a copy of mine?' Sure people can argue that more money can be saved by living together and for the most part they are right but everybody needs his or her own space. What better space can there be than your own? And not your own as in the extra room in the house you both share but your own as in 'I gotta get out of here, you're stressing me out – I'm going home.' Has a nice ring to it, doesn't it? How many times has there been this conversation?

'I don't like him in my house'
'but baby he's my oldest friend'
'well I don't trust him, find somewhere else to hang out!'

Everybody does not like every friend or relative of their significant other. How perfect would this be if people would never have to deal with a situation as above? Think about the potential perks; when there's an argument, instead of one person throwing the other out of the bedroom or out of the home, each party can go to their homes similar to the way boxers go to their respective corners during a fight. If you had to fight and then stay in the same household, wouldn't seeing that person everyday just prolong the anger? Most people I ask about this seem to agree but they quickly follow it up with 'I don't think that I will be able to trust him or her by herself for too long.' My thing is if you are incapable of trust, why get into the relationship on a committed level in the first place? And the answer I continually seem to come up with is that people want a perfect relationship but 1.) Will never work toward achieving that perfect relationship and 2.) Some people do not realize that they are incapable of trusting others.

Now even though I believe that most relationships are bad, I do believe that many relationships are a pretty wonderful thing – if you have the right person. There are some people who feel that the right person is whoever says any and everything they want to hear. There are others who feel that the right person is a carbon copy of whoever is right for their best friend or sister or brother. Relationships are not bullshit. How people interpret them and what they accept regarding them are. A lot of people get into relationships because they have their own individual twisted list of criteria when it comes to what actually defines or constitutes a relationship. **Here's where more bullshit comes in:** As stated above, an individual may base his or her prospective relationship on the actual relationship of someone else. This may mean that because one couple does a, b and c and claim to be in love, the prospective couple has to do the exact same thing to be in love also – otherwise the belief may exist that they are not completely in love. Here's an example: couple a can buy each other diamond rings to prove their love. Couple b, who does not make as much as couple a cannot buy diamond rings but instead of ½ of couple b understanding this and accepting the fact that love is more than monetary possessions, this person garners the belief that he or she is not loved as much as couple a. That sounds like bullshit to me but this is how many in relationships feel their relationships should go.

I remember mentioning in one of my other works when talking about relationships how if a couple were truly in love, then the value of the rings would not matter at all. A person could give the other a ring made out of bamboo and he or she would be as happy and as satisfied as if it were the biggest, most expensive diamond ring in existence. But this idea is little more than an extreme amount of wishful thinking because if the average individual was to give his significant other a ring, which has little to no monetary value, that person would lose his or her fucking mind. I mean really ask yourself; if your significant other said that his or her love for you could only be passed by the love of God and this person gave you a ring made out of bamboo or even copper as a symbol of their love, would you be just as satisfied? Or would you be temporarily satisfied as in, I will accept this now but later I want some ice in this ring? I'm guessing that most of the individuals in the civilized world would expect something of a higher monetary value and this is because of how important money is. People honestly will not be able to show their true colors, meaning what they really want and desire in a relationship until they are in a situation where they have all the money they will ever need or they don't have any money at all. This is a prime example of some of the bullshit in relationships. The average individual will equate love with the amount of money, which is spent, the same way the average individual will equate someone having a good job with prior college attendance. Neither of these scenarios has to be true. Another thing about relationships, which I find to be bullshit, is the fact that people cannot be truthful to their partners – if one says to the other I do not like you drinking, and the other does not want to or cannot stop, he or she may continue but hide the drinking to continue in the relationship. Instead of a person saying this is me, take it or leave it, this person will lie and hide things for the continuance of the relationship. People expect that if there is a problem in the relationship that the other is causing, then all that's necessary to correct that problem is for the other to stop doing what he or she is doing but this creates another problem. People can only change when they want to and not when somebody else wants them to which is why cheating will always be a problem in some relationships. I've noticed that when many people get caught cheating, they say that they will never do it again – and the main reason they say this is because they want to keep the relationship they have and because it is exactly what the other party wants to hear. But this is nothing more than a temporary pacification because until the cheating party finds what caused him or her to cheat and then fixes whatever it was that caused him or her to cheat, the cheating will more than likely happen again and again and again.

In regard to people in relationships not being completely truthful about what it is they want in their relationships, many couples will never reach the feeling of ultimate closeness and understanding because they are afraid to hurt the other's feelings or because they are afraid to have the other think that they are in any way less than perfect. This comes about by them not expressing to the other what they honestly and truly want for themselves and for the relationship. Here's a not too hypothetical example: there are several cruise lines, which offer clothing optional cruises. There are also many couples that like to indulge in activities of this sort. This is not the problem. Although these couples like to indulge in activities of this sort, they do so either without the significant other or without the significant other's knowledge. That's the problem. So what ends up happening is the couple never knows what the other REALLY likes or desires because they are too afraid to expose themselves as possible freaks or possible closet sadists or worst case scenario; possibly the exact same type of person that their significant other is. On a personal note, I have dated a few women who, after we had parted ways, mentioned to me that they didn't know I liked to do that...or they didn't think I would be the type to do this or that. We won't mention what the this or that was but the fact of the matter is that the complete and unbiased communication was not there. This is one of the reasons why couples cannot be completely honest with their partners and also one of the reasons why many relationships fail. This is one of the basic bullshit contradictions that life has for people in relationships. In life, people are taught that for success and happiness, they must be themselves. They must not act like someone whom they are not. Okay, I agree with that. But in relationships, for success, people are told rather taught that they have to assimilate themselves into whomever it is that the other person wants them to be for a happy relationship. Do you see the bullshit? If people were actually themselves in relationships, I believe more than half of those relationships would end. And this is not because people don't like everything about the person they are involved with. To do that would be impossible. It is because these people try to be something they're not, just so that the other person will like them.

This causes people to be fake. This causes people to like what is fake and most importantly, this causes fake relationships.

One last facet of bullshit that I would like to touch on is how many people focus too much sometimes on their significant others that they totally neglect everything else in their lives. This is what I like to call the tunnel vision effect. A good example of this would be the one of how some people who are in a relationship attend the same religious institution until they break up, then one doesn't go any more. That's some real bullshit there. Let me see if I got this right. People in a relationship can go to church, a place where everybody is supposed to be friends, a place of refuge, a place of problem solving and even worst case scenario, relationship help and correction – yet when there arises a seemingly insurmountable relationship problem which causes the couple of church goers to break up, they can no longer attend the same church? That sounds like some real bullshit to me. That sounds like someone has put their relationship above their faith. That sounds like instead of relying on a chosen higher power to settle their disputes, they are choosing to turn their backs on their chosen higher power. This is some more of the bullshit that exists in many relationships – especially those in a religious situation. I have known and even dealt with some people who were 'religious' and after a breakup, instead of going to clergy or their chosen higher power, these individuals would go and sleep with the first individual who came along. Never mind the fact that cheating was many times the issue, which caused the relationship to fail, these hurt people just bypassed the option that they should have taken for the one that they wanted to take. These so called religious folk instead of praying about it, rationalized it as an eye for an eye and said I want you to see how it feels. I ask you – is this how a relationship is supposed to go? Of course not – yet this is just another facet of the massive amount of bullshit that many in relationships are on. Many people are taught when someone hurts you the only recourse you have is to hurt them back. Now this strategy works well in schoolyard playgrounds but it rarely has the same success rate in the home. People have to forgive when involved in relationships but the problem is that many of these people who are in relationships have the schoolyard mentality. They do not completely understand that a real relationship, not these soap opera or reality show inspired farces, will have bouts of adversity which cannot just be thrown away. They will have to be overcome and the method of overcoming the obstacles of adversity will take much more work than just the eye for an eye mindset.

On Child Support

The idea behind child support, as told to me is the ongoing practice for a periodic payment made directly or indirectly by an 'obligor' to an 'obligee' for the financial care and support of children of a relationship or marriage that has been terminated or in some cases never existed. In laymen's terms, this simply means that a parent who does not have custody of the child will have to pay money to the parent who does have custody of the child. **Now here comes the bullshit:** The parent who does not have the child has to pay somewhere around 17% of his or her salary, not to the child but to child support. (Funny I don't remember <u>fucking</u> child support!) In addition to that, quite often that does not even guarantee that parent the privilege of seeing his or her child. Now let's do the math; if a person who had to pay child support only made a grand total of $100 and was ordered to pay 17% of that, unless I'm mistaken, wouldn't that come out to about $17? Now that may be good for the parent who has to pay it because that amount of money is basically the equivalent of a decent bottle of wine or a halfway decent pair of jeans but here's the logical and at the same time ridiculous question I have: how in the fuck can that amount do anything positive for a child? Now I am sure that most grown ups who are citizens and not incarcerated, make more than $100 a week. I am also aware that sometimes these people who have to indulge in this dreaded practice sometimes lose their jobs. **Now here comes some more bullshit:** when these people lose their jobs, they do not lose the privilege of paying child support. In fact the payments continue to accrue until these people get new jobs and are able to resume their prior payment plan. But here's the sad thing – sometimes it takes a few months or longer for someone to find a job. During this 'few months or longer' the missed payments can double, triple and quadruple in size. Now what sometimes occurs is the wonderful police assume that the people who lose their ability to make timely payments are nothing more than low life's, deadbeats and any other derogatory term they can think of and they set out on an 'arrest these motherfuckers at any cost' crusade because of that fact. Now I don't want anybody to believe that everybody who falls behind on their child support payments is an honest law abiding citizen who has just fallen on hard times because we all know that that is not true. Some parents out here just do not give half a fuck about their kids and feel that the only way they can cause detriment to the child's parent is by withholding the $$$$. Shame on them! What they don't always realize is that by using this method, more often than not, this is causing the custodial parent of the child to become more and more upset with the non custodial parent which will more often than not cause the custodial parent to curse out the non custodial parent and often in front of the child which will eventually lead that child to believe the hurtful and disheartening things that the custodial parent fills his or her little head up with. My question is why, instead of this child support façade, why can't there be a more novel idea, like say maybe time support? By this I simply mean instead of demanding that a person pay x amount of dollars to some mysterious agency that is supposed to be providing adequately for this person's child, why can't these stupid ass judges demand that a parent spend x amount of time with their offspring? I mean isn't that the real meaning of child support - supporting a child? There is no way a person, man or woman, can be an adequate parental figure if their only means of interaction in their offspring's life is financial. I mean sure having money to provide for everything a child may desire is a definite good thing but it is not the only thing and this is what I try to get across to many people who feel I am wrong for my hatred of the whole child support system. When people are only required to involve themselves monetarily, the impression is given that nothing else they can provide is necessary or desired. In other words 'all I need is your wallet or purse. I don't need your sympathy, I don't need you to help put the child to bed at night, I don't need you to tell the child you love him or her, I don't need you to take the child to a doctor's appointment.' 'I don't even need you to acknowledge the child.' This impression is unfortunately given by not only the custodial parent of the child, but more so by the agencies that demand it.

In addition to this, there will always be an abundance of dumb dick motherfuckers who will more than emphatically proclaim that they are 'good' parents because their child support payments are and always have been up to date. That is 'good' probably for their credit rating or maybe their conscience but how does it help the child? If a child does not know his mother or father but receives a check from this individual, the child may be under the mistaken impression that the mother or father did not want to be in the child's life at all and in addition to that, the wonderfully perceptive child may actually believe that he or she is somehow responsible for the parent's decision to not remain in the child's life. This is one of those impressions that sometimes take years and years to dispel – especially if the custodial parent is one of those who offer a healthy dose of 'your mother or father ain't shit' every so often. As mentioned previously, when you give money and nothing else, you are seen as only being 'good' for giving money and nothing else. This child support thing is pretty much a no win situation because if you don't pay it, you're wrong and if you do pay it, you're equally wrong. So my question is, other than making a peaceful and happy existence for those who have to pay it almost impossible, what purpose does it really serve? Not to mention that when the average individual walks into the average child support office, these trifling bastards ask you for all of your information pertaining to your case just to see what your status is and by status, I mean whether or not your account is in good standing – and they do this before even asking how may I help you? If your account is not in good standing, whether because an individual has lost a job or whether an individual is a lowlife deadbeat who has no intention or concern of taking care of his or her children, they will willingly inform you by saying and I quote 'you owe one, two or three thousand dollars.' Is this proper protocol or are these the same type of bullshit tactics that the bill collectors use when they call? I don't care what anybody says, the child support system is not geared toward those who have to pay it. It is not geared toward the children who are supposed to receive it. It is split between toward the city agencies that oversee it and the custodial parents who more often than not do things with it other than its intended purpose which if anyone has forgotten, is to help take care of the child – hence the term child SUPPORT.

On Child Custody

In the time since bullshit records have been kept, I honestly believe that there is no truer and exasperatingly stupid form of bullshit than this. According to the laws of some retarded, backwards thinking society, the belief is in place that children from a couple who has broken up, fare better with the mother after the break up. They say ignorant things like 'a child belongs with his or her mother' but my thing is if a child has two parents, then why is one all of a sudden unable to be the parent of the child just because their relationship has come to an end? Another facet of this bullshit, rather another facet of this ginormous level of bullshit is the thing about if a couple is in the process of breaking up and a young child is taken by one of the parents, the other parent has to go to court to get that child back or even see said child. Now I know that there are some of you who may say that my views on this issue are somewhat controversial, harsh and maybe even wrong but I had to deal with this shit and forgive me for my feelings but I am still trying to extricate the logic from this equation. People in our esteemed court system have this dumb ass belief of 'the best interests for the child.' They feel that since the parents are experiencing some sort of adversity or turmoil in their relationship, they cannot be effective in raising a happy, healthy and or productive child together, so they attempt to determine which of the two will be the most positively influential figure for the child or if not that, then they attempt to figure a way in which both parents can have equal or at least partial involvement in the child's life. Now by most sensible accounts, this would be an excellent method of determination when it comes to how time is shared but the way in which these asinine agencies, such as family court, make these determinations on who a child is better off with is pure bullshit. My thing is how can any reasonable individual or entity for that matter, make the assumption that a child's best interests will be better suited by the type of job the parent has or even if the parent has a job at all for that matter? I am fully aware of the fact that a child needs to have contact or at least knowledge of both parents even if one is not doing as legally well or as morally well as the other but my thing is how can anybody make that determination based on only a few hours or a few weeks of observation, the way some of these entities who determine which parent a child is going to be placed with do? You see, this is the bullshit, which causes animosity. This is the bullshit, which causes confusion in the eyes of the child. This causes parents to lie to the children – sometimes to the effect of 'your mother or father doesn't love you' when in actuality it is 'some stupid ass judge or legal equivalent has determined that you have to stay with me instead of the mother or father whom you love.'

On Security

This might very well be the biggest contradiction ever invented. I have worked in the contract security field for well over sixteen years and after gaining all the experience I have gained, meeting all of the people I have met and traveled to all of the locations I have had the pleasure of travelling to, I have come to the grand conclusion that contract security is bullshit. I call contract security a contradiction because of many reasons. The first is the very definition of the word security. Security means (and I'm going by the dictionary definition) safety, refuge, sanctuary and safekeeping. Through my illustrious almost twenty year security career, I found that basically none of those descriptions applied to my field of work at all. From my understanding and experience, the job of the security officer is to observe and report. This does not mean protect, defend or help when in trouble. This means that a security officer is supposed to stand there or sit there depending upon the organization's protocol and watch something happen, then tell somebody. So let me see if I can put this in the proper perspective for you. According to the contract security job description, if a person is getting the you know what beat out of them, then all the security officer is <u>allowed</u> to do is call the police. The security officer is not supposed to get off his or her behind because (from what I've come to understand) the company will be liable if the security officer violates the rights of the person beating up the other. As if that weren't bad enough, the person getting beat up could sue the security officer for helping him in the first place. I know this may sound a little strange so I'll break it down a little bit more for you. Let's say that on a nice bright sunny day, an individual is sitting in the park using his laptop and some not raised right individual decides to try and steal the laptop from the other. The not raised right individual manages to procure the laptop from its owner. The contract security officer who just happens to be stationed in the park sees the struggle between the two individuals and intervenes. The security officer takes the laptop away from the not raised right individual and bashes him over the head with it about ten or fifteen times. The not raised right individual runs away and the laptop is returned to the rightful owner. Sounds like all is well, right? Wrong. What happened was…the next day the not raised right individual ends up in the hospital. He has a concussion. Not only does he have a concussion but the doctor that treated him has a best friend who is an 'in between cases' personal injury lawyer. After 'fixing' the concussion and 'fixing' the story about how the over zealous security officer attacked him as he was returning the laptop to the rightful owner who forgot it in the park, a lawsuit is filed against the security officer's organization as well as the security officer. Now if that wasn't bad enough, it had come to be found out that the individual's laptop, who the good Samaritan security officer had fought so diligently to save has a cracked screen and according to the individual, has lost all of the irreplaceable information because the hard drive was irreparably damaged and needs to be replaced. So now the security officer who was just doing what most people would want a security officer to do has just lost his job because of the lawsuit. He is also getting sued himself and has to pay for somebody to receive a brand new laptop. The security officer is in a pretty bad situation or as they say, between a rock and a hard place because if he does his job, which is just to watch and call the cops then he will be thought of and referred to as a worthless individual – to wit: 'somebody beat me up, stole my laptop and the security officer just stood right there.' If he doesn't do his job and tries to intervene, he is setting himself up for a boatload of possible trouble. From my experience, the company that employs this security officer will not in any way back him up in defending against the lawsuit. In fact many contract companies will distance themselves from the employee as if he were a ten dollar prostitute and the company was a man who had just had sex with her.

Another reason why I call this 'profession' a contradiction is because of what many security guard companies put in their training manuals when hiring new officers and that is the little stipulation that you are supposed to protect people and property but you don't have any arrest powers or as many companies put it 'a security officer has the same powers as an ordinary citizen. Let's examine that for a second. In ALL of the contract security officer jobs I have had, it was either expressly implied or outright stated that a security officer has the same powers as an ordinary citizen - which basically means that if an ordinary citizen were to put on a security officer uniform, and attend a class for eight hours, not pay attention but attend, then wala! He's a security officer. When you think of it like that, contract security officers don't really have jobs – at least not important ones. Now there is (thanks to the security guard act of I believe 1992 – don't quote me!) protocol, which requires all security officers to be licensed and trained in their respective fields of employment. I think this is more bullshit because much of the things, which are taught in the security training classes are rarely if at all used on the job. I remember when I first stated doing security and it was much different back then. I mean if people would get out of line, then they would be dealt with by security until the police arrived. Now people get out of line all the time and dare security to call the cops. There is no respect in this profession and that is because people know that many unarmed security officers have little to no power and this is not to say that the security officer is weak in strength. This is to say that many of them are weak when it comes to effectiveness. How can an individual really be effective when the public at large knows that the individual can only be but so effective? I think that contract security officers are hired (besides decoration) for those individuals who don't know what the limits of the security officer are. That way those people will listen to or respect the security officer based on what they believe he can do as well as how they were raised. If they believe that the security officer can arrest them, they will more than likely listen out of fear. If they were raised to respect authority, then maybe they will listen to the officer based on that fact. But here's the catch, many people know that the security officer has no real authority and many more people don't respect authority in any form. Now if people don't respect authority from parents or law enforcement, then what the hell is the lowly security officer going to do? Not a damn thing. The security officer is going to do whatever he can to ensure that he makes it home safely to his family. Now don't get me wrong; the last thing I mean to do is imply that all security guards are weak, scared or simpletons. I mean there are a lot of them out there but many more are what I like to call closet intelligents and by this I mean that these men and women know more about the security business and life in general than many of the supervisors and managers running amuck. I want people to realize that just because contract security for the most part has a negative, limp dick connotation associated with it, that does not mean that all security officers are retarded – a lot of these security guard companies are retarded but that doesn't always hold true for the individual. The belief that all security officers are the same, whether in intelligence or abilities is the real bullshit.

Okay we've covered the liability and the perception. Now's there's something else that all people don't seem to know about security officers and that is fact that many officers are viewed as targets because of their job description. It's a well known fact that many of the individuals who work in the field of security are from different countries and in these countries there is rarely the type of violence that exists in this country. Many of these officers in trying to do a good job as security often overstep their bounds and get victimized as a result and not only do they get victimized but they cause others to get victimized as well. Many people share this twisted kind of thinking which leads them to believe that all security officers are the same. So if one individual has a bad experience with a security officer and beats him up, he may feel that all security officers are deserving of a butt whipping as well. This is some real bull but this is how many people are. In addition to not respecting the uniform, these people feel that just because a security guard is such, he should get hurt. Crazy ain't it? But here's what's really crazy; in many of these security officer training classes, people are taught to keep a personal and professional distance from the people they work among – no fraternization. This in a sense is understandable because once a person makes friends on the job it becomes increasingly hard to get those people to follow orders. But here's the thing that many companies who instill this fraternization policy don't completely understand; when a person works among the general public, that person needs to make friends. That person needs to be personable and approachable because sooner or later that person will need some kind of help. It is much easier to receive help from people that like you as opposed to the opposite. When you do residential security for instance, chances are you will be dealing with many different types of mindsets and attitudes. In addition to that there is the fact that you will not be able to please everyone. What is likely going to happen when a person is mean to everyone they work among as many of these security companies' protocol dictates and they make a couple of enemies? Or what if a person is not mean at all but someone or maybe a few someone's interpret this individual's behavior as such? Will the security company come and drive this person home everyday? Of course not. But this is some of the bullshit that they want you to do. Security companies are quick to say 'don't make friends on the job' but the thing that a lot of these companies don't realize is that often the security officers live among the people they work around. And it's quite often a strong possibility that sooner rather than later, the security officer who made an enemy on the job will have to deal with that enemy after work or when he's with his family trying to enjoy the day off. Many of these higher ups in these companies don't live anywhere near the places they send the officers to and therefore don't have to worry about potential problems caused by the security officer doing his or her job. That's some real bullshit ain't it?

Okay now we've covered liability, perception and the fact that people easily become targets because of the job. Now let's talk about the tip security companies give to their officers. I'm sorry but I just can't bring myself to call the amount of money most of these contract security companies pay their employees a paycheck. As I mentioned before, I have been employed in this field for close to twenty years. When I first started doing security, the minimum wage was somewhere around $3.35 an hour. Now it's somewhere around $7 - $8per hour. (I forget which) The point I'm trying to make is that almost nobody over the age of eighteen can live on that unless you are talking about people who reside in third world countries. Yet that is what many of these companies expect and not only expect but expect their employees to do it with a smile. (Like they're supposed to be grateful that they have a job.) Here's the thing; many of these jobs which put the security officer's well being in jeopardy by forcing them to be everything a police officer should only pay either the minimum wage or not much above it. And then people have the audacity to wonder why the security officers never smile or always seem to have a less than sunny disposition. I have been asked many times why I am not thankful for the fact that I have a job and my response would always be - I am thankful, I just can't afford to live on the salary I am receiving. And there would always be without fail, some perpetually happy jackass saying something to the effect of 'at least you have a job' or 'a job is not only about the money.' I asked many of these people 'do you like the job you're presently doing?' And almost all of them answered yes. Yet when I asked these dopes 'would you do your job for my salary?' Their tunes changed quicker than shit. They couldn't wait to laugh in my face. They would start with the 'well I went to college and my education dictates that I make a certain amount' and all that other bullshit. They would continue with 'I have bills and responsibilities that your salary couldn't afford to take care of.' When I would mention to the assholes that I too, had bills and responsibilities that my salary could not take care of, they offered the advice of 'well then you need to get a better job.' And people wonder why I'm a smartass! Here's the bullshit; nobody wants to admit that when it comes to employment it is all about the money. If it wasn't, there would be about a hundred million more volunteers in this world. If it wasn't all about the money, then almost everybody in the employment world would work for minimum wage. But we know this will never happen. People just want to keep that professional distance so to speak from security. They know that security is extremely important because they are the ones who have to stay up all night and make sure that no unwanted individuals saunter into their building. They know that security has to keep an eye on their kids when they are too inattentive, too busy or too absent minded to do so. They know that security has to be that calming presence when they walk into their buildings late night or stagger in early morning drunk off their asses but here's the thing; they will only pay these security officers the bare minimum. They will expect that the security officer likes to do the job that he or she is doing. They will reward the security officer with leftover meals from the office party or from any random house party the building may have and if the security guard is lucky, he may even get a bottle of liquor for his efforts or for his silence. Security guards face so many unreported dangers daily - from walking up to suspected and known drug dealers and asking them to move out of an entranceway so that elderly people who are scared to can enter into their homes, to asking people who may or may not have volatile tempers to stop smoking weed and drinking and making noise because neighbors are complaining. Security officers have even been placed in known gang locations by themselves to keep peace and safety in the building. These security officers are expected to excel at access control and by this I mean that they are not supposed to let any unauthorized individuals into the location they are securing. Let's look at this for a second. If a security officer is working in a gang environment and let's just say that the building is one where there is heavy drug traffic or even let's just say that the building is one where drugs are being sold and the security officer is told to keep the doors closed and not let anyone in unless they have a key. What do you or any legitimately sensible person think is going to happen when that lowly security officer tries to do his job, which will more than likely be interpreted by those committing crimes and selling drugs and such as an attempt at stopping their flow of money? He will either get beat up, shot, or chased out of the building. But these employers have the fucking audacity to expect that after an eight hour or maybe even sixteen hour class in security guard protocol, that these people who may have never done security before, are ready to handle that and not only handle that but do so effectively. And as a reward for accomplishing all of this and more, without getting shot – or without getting the shit beat out of them, these security companies want to show their gratitude by tipping officers a measly seven to eight dollars an hour. That, my friends, is some real bullshit.

I am finding it increasingly difficult to end this topic on security and the bullshit it entails. One of the things or practices that many security companies seem to pretty much consistently indulge in is the practice of violating a person's rights when it comes to employment. Now in all of my almost thirty years of employment experience, I have come to believe and expect that for every eight hours a person is expected to work, that person is to receive a meal break. Now there are several discrepancies about how long this break is to be but a break is supposed to be had nonetheless. **Now here comes the bullshit:** if a person who is employed as a security officer just happens to work a particular shift – for this example, I will use the overnight shift, that person may or may not get a break – even though a break from my understanding, is required by law. I have had several jobs (including the one I am using now to write this book) which have this unwritten stipulation that states if you work at a location where you are the only security officer, and there is no one to relieve you, you are not to take a break. This is some real bullshit because even pigs – wait, sorry – cops, get a break so why can't security? I have been relieved from several of my duties as a security officer because of the above stated reason. I would take my own break when there was no one to relieve me and I was always under the impression that if I were to ever get fired for being off post, the law would have my back. Silly me. I slowly came to the realization that security companies can fire you – even if they are the ones breaking the law. That's some real bullshit. Kinda drives home the point of how much importance there is regarding ones' job again, doesn't it? I know that there are some legal eagles out there who are probably saying 'well why didn't you file a lawsuit against the company for such a blatant disregard of your rights?' Well for you legal eagles, I did. And I was enlightened by the new and highly effective process that these security companies use as a response to those who actually take the time and consult a lawyer. The companies change the fucking name of the company. I had come to find out that a lawsuit is completely ineffective against a company, which does not exist. In other words, if a company receives a lawsuit because of the bullshit that they are perpetrating, then as long as the sued company gets a new business name within a timely fashion, the lawsuit will be null & void. Ain't that some shit?

On The Penal System

I believe the idea behind the penal system is a wonderful thing. The penal system was created (in my opinion) to remove certain individuals from society who were either a threat to society or generally unable to exist peacefully in society. It was created (again in my opinion) to house violent and sometimes non violent offenders of the law in a mutually 'supportive' environment. **Now here comes the bullshit:** There is an enormous amount of talk about the main purpose or rather one of the main purposes of the job of the penal system is rehabilitation of suspected and actual criminals. If this were actually true, wouldn't it be much more feasible if education was a mandate instead of just an option? Think about this for a second. If prisoners were forced to get their college degrees and or high school diplomas and or even learn their ABC's, wouldn't that possibly make for a better or at least more intelligent individual upon their release? Think about something else: if prisoners were taught the marketable skills and people skills necessary to obtain and maintain employment, would there be such a high return rate? I think not. The reason I saw these individuals should be forced into education and skills training is because apparently many of them are not that good decision makers when it comes to choosing positive career paths. If they were, would so many of them be in jail in the first place? Again, I think not. Now I know there are some instances where these over zealous and over retarded officers of the law falsely and incorrectly put away the wrong individuals but I do believe that to be strongly in the minority. Some people just do wrong because they either know no better or because they think that they know better than everybody else. Rehabilitation is defined as restoring something or someone back to normal. However when the word is applied to individuals in the penal system, rehabullashit is a much more apt description. When an individual takes a look at the preponderance of return inmates and revolving door inmates, (those who come out of jail and go right back in and then get out and repeat the process) it is extremely hard to fathom that the rehabilitation of these individuals was an overwhelming success. What an individual will most likely fathom is that the whole penal system façade is nothing more than an excuse to group individuals into one classification and lock them away for as long as the law allows. This way the 'nice' people will not have to deal with those individuals who are misunderstood, mis-trained and misinformed as to the ways of society. In other words, the powers that be would rather lock these individuals up and throw away the key based on the infractions they commit. I think that is some real bullshit. What I think is even more bullshit is this thing of locking away prisoners for some twenty three hours a day with only one hour of recreation. That is inhumane. No matter what crimes these individuals commit, they are still human beings. You cannot lock someone up like that for years upon years and expect him to be in any way normal. My thing is if they are going to be in jail for the rest of their lives and the sentence dictates or mandates that they be locked in a cell for twenty three hours, then just kill the motherfuckers. I mean think about it; they're not going to get out anyway. In addition to that there is always all of this talk about how the prisons are overcrowded and such. My plan would basically eliminate that and mighty quickly I might add. If people cause such a threat to themselves or others that they cannot be amongst other human beings, then put a fucking bullet in their skulls and be done with them. Stop all this bullshit about people having rights and shit. How can you say that people have rights when you are basically treating them as less than a slave? I know people commit horrible and horrendous crimes all the time and the powers that be often sentence these offenders to either death or life imprisonment. The death I can fully understand but life? That shit makes no sense whatsoever. If an individual does something so awful where he or she is slated to die, have a firing squad right outside the courtroom and blast that ass to kingdome come. But if people commit crimes and are sentenced to life in prison, they may actually become accustomed to life on the inside and not only that, they may actually enjoy being there. From my understanding, prison was never meant to be a daycare. It was never meant to be a summer or winter retreat either. It was meant to be a punishment for the dregs of society who violate the laws of society that law abiding members of society follow. Think about what may possibly happen if say one hundred or so people get sentenced to life in prison and they become acclimated to the lifestyle and they live for about fifty or sixty years. That would mean that one hundred or so criminals would be clogging up the penal system for those fifty or sixty years and at the same time contributing to the massive overcrowding in our jails today. If you go with my plan and just shoot these motherfuckers, the potential problem would be solved and people on the outside would more than likely think two, three and four times before they commit crimes if they knew they could die for their actions. Now I know there is the thing about appeals and all that shit but that could be eliminated by more competent lawyers and less corrupt law enforcement personnel. Then the criminal justice system and the penal system would actually be effective. It would not be seen as a joke. It would not be something that inner city kids would use to prove their manhood. So many of these people who have never been to college or who have never had any legal training know so much about the legal process that it's no wonder they challenge it at every given opportunity. They know that if they do this crime, they will get only a couple of months. They know that if they do that crime, they can get up to a year, and so forth. There would not be all of this commissary shit. There would not be all of this gang violence, where prisoners overtake the institutions. There would not be all of this money being used to take care of prisoners who are being treated like they are not being taken care of at all. There would not be family members having to take time out of their busy schedules to come and basically be treated like a prisoner themselves before they can come and visit their loved ones on the inside. I tell you boy, if I had my way, things would be a lot different.

Another way I believe the penal system could be improved is by eliminating all of these baby jails and preparatory jails and just make every new institution, which is built follow the same design and housing structure as the supermax prisons. In other words, no county jail. No central booking. Just incarceration with the worst of the worst. Think about the mindset of many of the people who commit crimes these days. Many of them do so because they know the ramifications of their actions. They know that they an only receive so much time for so much crime so they commit the crimes. If it were a situation of whatever crime they were convicted of they would have to serve their time in a prison which houses people who are there for life, people who kill other inmates, people who rape other inmates and people who do things that you don't hear about on the news, I'm sure these people would think two, three, four and five times about the crimes they wanted to commit. But see, this is why the penal system is looked at as a joke sometimes. Criminals know how to manipulate it.

Lawyers know how to manipulate it. If people knew that for carrying around an unlicensed firearm, instead of doing a few months on Rikers island, they were going to Colorado to spend those few months at a supermax facility, I'm pretty sure damn near all of them would stop doing the dumb shit they do.

Continuing with some of the bullshit that the penal system is famous for, there is something which is not exactly a factor relating to the penal system but a method in which many individuals avoid having to deal with the penal system. It is called the insanity defense. People have been embroiled in this never seeming to end debate about whether the insanity defense is actually valid. I believe I can clear this debate up in about one second. It's not! Insanity is bullshit in its purest form. And those who pull this defense off are clever to the likes of the greatest magicians that history has ever shown. I believe that insanity is not perpetrated. I believe that people do things, after which, they realize that they have went into fubar status, fucked up beyond all repair, and then they say if I fuck up even more, the powers that be will have but no other choice but to believe I'm crazy and let me go free or to a safe institution. A prime example of this is when somebody kills another, whether intentionally or accidentally and they fathom that there is no chance for them to ever escape the consequences, which are about to befall them. They then chop up and eat the body or they hide the body under their bed and or set out plates of food for the dead person to eat. Okay now these are extreme and completely, well mostly made up examples but they show that when a person messes up really badly, the best way to help that person's case is to make it seem like what that person has done is something that he or she believes is normal but at the same time as completely far away from what an otherwise normal person would ever do. I believe that there are exceptions for this bullshit defense and those exceptions would be those who are defined as developmentally disabled or people who have been either in institutions before or been previously classified as having some sever mental disorder before any crime was ever committed. People who are not crazy will stab another over one hundred times. Why would they do this? Because after the first or first few stabs when they realize that 'oh shit this motherfucker I dead, I can go to jail for this' they continue to stab so that in the mind of the people who are trying to establish this individual's guilt or innocence will be the thought of 'no sensible person would have done something like this, he has to be crazy.' This is the game that people in certain situations play. They play this game of bullshit so that they do not have to endure the bigger bullshit, which is the penal system. If all of the people who claimed the insanity defense were actually crazy, they wouldn't be allowed to drive cars. They wouldn't be allowed to have kids. They wouldn't be allowed to walk the streets for fear of them doing something crazy on a whim. The one thing about crazy people, which I believe to be universal, is the fact that everybody who is usually around them knows that they are crazy. There is no sociopath thing where one day they just flip and kill 360 people. Everybody knows that a crazy person is crazy except that crazy person himself. But what people continue to do is accept this bullshit and let killers go free or get sent to a country club like mental institution on the simple fact that they know how to manipulate the system. That's bullshit. But then again, what's the title of this book?

On Emotions

Emotions are those little things, which characterize an individual's state of mind. Most often they are referred to simply as feelings. I sincerely believe that there is no stronger force in this world than that of emotion especially since they entail things such as love and hate. Unfortunately many people in this world do not give emotions the respect they deserve. Let's examine the emotion of love for a second. When people are driven by their interpretation of love, they will often do things, which can be characterized as wonderful, stupid, extravagant or even crazy, to name a few. An example of this could be the multi million dollar rings that many celebrities have been rumored to give to their significant others. Now does this mean that these celebrities love their significant others any more than you or I, or does it mean that these celebrities have any conceptual idea of word the word love actually entails? Of course not. What it could mean is that they want their significant others as well as the world at large to believe that they do. You see, some people have this belief that love means doing any and everything for the significant other. I have to say that I am inclined to agree – but note, there are stipulations. Some people who believe as above, that love has no limit, will attempt to prove that by purchasing things to show their affection that nobody else in their right mind would or even could afford. Again, this could be deception or it could be an individual's attempt to show how they react to stimulations of their emotions.

Now let's examine the emotion of hate. People are quick to say that hate is a strong word. People say that you should not use that word because the ramifications of doing so could lead to sometimes irreversible consequences. When people are driven by the emotion of hate, rarely is there room left for logical thought. People react because others or other things have made them so angry that they feel their only recourse is to hate. The main difference between the love and hate emotions is that when people act on their interpretation of love, it can often be confused with a multitude of other things – such as infatuation, impulsiveness or even desperation. On the other hand, when people act or react to their interpretations of hate, it is confused with nothing. People have a pretty good idea when others do not like them.

Now here comes the bullshit: Many people in this world think that emotions vary according to gender. In other words if you are a man, you are not allowed to show or be in touch with your emotions but if you are a woman, then the exact opposite is true. This is bullshit. In fact this might even be among the highest level of bullshit that I can immediately think of and the reason why is simply because everybody has emotions and reacts to or is affected by their own as well as everybody else's emotions at some time or another. Emotions, just like relationships, are not bullshit. How people interpret them are. People really have to ask themselves, is every man who cries any less of a man who doesn't? Society has basically made it a crime for a man to show emotion unless it is a hateful or aggressive one. But here comes the hypocrisy; many women who get into relationships want men to show emotion. And here comes even more hypocrisy; the emotion, which is shown, can only be shown during certain times. Here's a for instance: during a funeral, people are expected to grieve. This includes both, men and women. So when a man cries at the loss of a loved one, nobody really raises an eyebrow. In fact, the more a man shows emotion, the more love there is or was between him and the departed or so is the belief. Now if a man were to lose say a smart phone and cry over it or even shedding a tear over a so called chick flick, that man would lose his man card, so to speak. He would be classified as a straight up bitch and why? It's because people are taught that emotions are to be suppressed if you are one gender but embraced if you are another. Now this is one of the reasons why communication is a problem in many relationships. All men are not really taught how to get in touch with their feelings. They are most often taught that if a woman wants to leave, then just say fuck that bitch and let her go. Rarely are they taught that it's okay to say boo hoo, I love you and I don't want you to leave. And why, because everybody and their mother – especially and including the woman who is about to leave will probably be saying 'he started crying like a little bitch.' People are scared of classifications. That's why they can't be truthful with themselves or others. If nobody in this world cared whether a man cried or not, then I believe that every man would. There was even a book by a famous author called Men Cry In The Dark. Now I have never read the book but look at the title. I may be wrong but from my interpretation, it implies that some men are scared to show emotion to women. This façade is what causes relationships to fail. This title shows that when no one is around, men are human too. On a personal note and at the risk of one or more of you fake thug types classifying me as less than a man, I am secure enough to admit that there have been at least a couple of instances where I have cried in front of a woman. One of those was during a so called chick flick. The flick was Titanic and the scene was when Kate Winslet actually left the safety of her lifeboat to find her narrow ass boyfriend. The reason why I found that scene so emotional was because that is what I envision true love to actually entail number one and number two, I have yet to find a woman who would actually do that shit for my narrow ass! Think about that for a second; people are always throwing around the I love you's and the I will do anything for you's and the I will die for you's but how many people will actually risk their lives for a significant other? I don't believe that many and the reason is because many of the relationships in this world are fake. People will say I'll do anything for you just as long as it doesn't jeopardize my safety. Thinking about the last example with Kate and the lifeboat, I could just hear my significant other right now if I were to tell her to get on the lifeboat and I would see her back on dry land. She probably wouldn't wait until I finished the sentence! I'd be like 'okay honey, careful getting on the lifebo-' and she'd be like 'bye motherfucker!'

Emotions are dangerous. There was a case recently about a young lady, an astronaut, who was charge with attempted murder of a romantic rival. The media reported that the astronaut drove some 900 miles wearing a diaper or diapers – I'm not sure which, so that she would not have to stop and I guess use the bathroom. Now I'm sure that the majority of you will agree that this is crazy. But do you see how dangerous this actually is? A woman has had her emotions riled to the point where she would actually drive across country to do something – I don't know what but something to someone else? That is beyond dangerous. When people are not in control of their emotions, things like this and worse occur.

On Identification

With billions of people walking the face of the earth, I believe the idea of being able to know who people are and where they come from is a good thing. In fact when you think about the potential damage which could be done both on a grand scale, such as a terroristic act and on a small scale, as with a personal relationship, it is a great thing.

Now here comes the bullshit: An identification card or id as it is more commonly known, is supposed to be for the identifying of individuals. It is supposed to let others know who a person is, aid in the apprehension of criminals as well as provide proof of an individual's age so that that individual can indulge in adult only activities. But as of late the reasoning behind its existence has leaped from knowing whom a person is, straight to just cause for locking up someone who has mistakenly forgotten it on his or her dresser. Id's are good because as stated before, they can help to let people know who is who. They can let law enforcement know who has a warrant, who is doing underage drinking or who is breaking curfew. With some of these new Internet companies, a person can take another's id and check his or her background as well as that person's credit. The bad thing about a person's id is that if a person were to lose it, anybody else with half an ounce of brains and deception could become that person. One of the other bad things about an identification card is the fact that many of them contain a person's home address. Just think for a minute what if someone with psychotic tendencies found or stole the id card of a female he was interested in? This person would be able to follow, stalk or appear at the targeted individual's home at any time. All thanks to a lost id card. Now I am not saying that people need to stop carrying identification to lessen the likelihood of unwelcome interaction with some crazy person. That type of interaction could be avoided or lessened by people paying more attention to their possessions. Now the real bullshit about identification cards comes about with the expiration dates. Personally, I have missed out on several offers of employment because my id card was one day beyond the expiration date. Now this is some real bullshit because I am still the same person. Somebody please explain to me how this is in any way a feasible law? If a person has an id card on Monday and its expiration date is on Tuesday, what is the big deal about it still being able to be used on Tuesday? I can completely understand if the id were five or six years old but one godforsaken day? Come on now. I have always tried to be a logical thinking person and my logic is leading me to believe that the whole id thing is all about money. Seriously, what else could it be? If you don't walk around with an id card, they take you to jail. If you do walk around with an id card which is past the date printed on the card itself, then legally you are not who you say you are. That's some bullshit.

On The Debt

Since about as far back as I can even begin to remember, there has been this thing called the national debt. And with just about every election I can seem to remember, the powers that be have placed the dubious honor and responsibility of handling this debt on the man who is elected every few years as president. **Now here comes the bullshit:** The debt is still here. Why blame the president? Realistically, he can't do much about it. I mean honestly, not to discount all of the excellent and good things that all of our present and past presidents have done to keep this country as great as it has been but if one man could actually solve the debt crisis, wouldn't it have been solved already? Here's one of my wonderful yet almost always underrated suggestions at work: why can't these not rich but super rich people and corporations be forced to contribute a certain amount every so often to help eradicate or at least reduce this debt? I know there is a plan and all to tax the rich but what if there was such a thing as forceful donations? I know it may sound a little harsh and primeval but bear with me. If these corporations and individuals who made billions and billions of dollars – not in their lifetimes and existences but per year were 'forced' to contribute say about a few million each year, wouldn't that put a somewhat significant dent in this already out of control debt? Let's hypothetically say that all entities, business and personal, who amassed more than a billion dollars was 'forced' to contribute a million or so for every billion they have toward the debt every year – and the millionaires were 'forced' to give around ten percent of their fortunes as well? We could knock this debt out or at least down to manageable status in record time or so one would think. I would like for all of the logical people in this world to think about something for a second. Billionaires have more money than they can logically spend. Am I wrong? If so I defy any billionaire to prove me so. I mean the only way I can fathom a person spending a billion dollars is foolishly. Once the family is taken care of and those dream purchases are purchased, other than acting like a philanthropist and giving it away or opening educational institutions in third world countries or something of that magnitude, what else is there to do? I mean sure you could take a trip into outer space or even purchase your own island but after that, the questions still remain. In many churches, there is the practice of giving tides. This amounts to donating 10% of your salary to the church. If an individual made $100 per week, then he or she would be asked to give $10. This by no means will make or break anyone I know of – so why can't it be done with those individuals who make more money than they will ever be able to spend? I'll tell you why. It's because people have become so accustomed to looking out for number one that they have compartmentalized their thinking into 'if I help you, it will hurt me, therefore I am not going to help you.' This is supposed to be the greatest country in the history of countries. How can it remain great if the people who live here don't want to help it remain that way? Let's go a little further with this tides type of thinking for a second. What if this idea could be applied to all working people, ten percent of their salaries going toward this supposedly inescapable debt? In a few years this debt would be non existent. And just think for a second if this country had little to no debt to worry about. How much money could be left over for necessary programs? I'm guessing a whole fucking lot! Let's think about the homeless situation for a second; living in NYC, I encounter someone who is homeless or who appears to be homeless almost daily. Sometimes I encounter between five and ten homeless individuals on my commute to work and mind you, it's only a forty minute commute. Whenever I can I will 'donate' a dollar or two to these individuals so that they can do something to help their situation. Now granted, a dollar or two can't do much but it can at the very least help someone get something to put in their stomachs. I have even encountered individuals who possessed an odor so bad that it made my stomach turn. I know in my heart that a few dollars would not help these individuals. Why? Simple – where in the hell could they spend it? I've done a little research and found that according to published reports, the highest billionaires are holding on to somewhere around sixty or seventy billion dollars. If these billionaires would ban together and put forth an effort, scratch that – put forth an honest effort at ending this homeless thing, the homeless thing would not stand a chance. But again the problem with people is that all too often, they think about themselves. They think how can what I'm doing help me. This is the bullshit. I remember one time seeing an individual give a homeless person a twenty dollar bill on the train. The homeless man was overjoyed. I was happy for him. Most people would never do that because they are too busy thinking about what this homeless person would probably do with that money. Many in our very judgmental society would say he's probably going to use that money for drugs or alcohol and therefore I'm am not going to help support his habit. This is more bullshit. Nobody knows what anybody out here is going through. And it's nobody's position to play judge or jury in regard to how their lives are lived. Think about it – if everybody had twenty bucks to give to every homeless person they encounter, there probably wouldn't be a hungry or smelly beyond belief, homeless person walking around. But people won't do that. People are scared to do that. People would rather spend that twenty dollars on drugs or alcohol for themselves instead of thinking that maybe the homeless man or woman may actually have a family who needs that money. If you think about it, twenty dollars goes into a billion a whole lotta damn times. Just like the debt, this homeless thing can be controlled. People need to work together and change their thinking. This me against the world mindset is what's killing this world.

On This Minimum Wage Thing

Minimum wage from my understanding is supposed to be the lowest amount of money that can be paid to an individual who performs work or a related service. I may be wrong but I believe the invention of minimum wage was so that individuals with little to no education can work and receive a livable wage. **Now here comes the bullshit:** The minimum wage is not something people can live on. It is something that people can exist on. And yes there is a difference between the two. When it comes to existing, people can exist on anything. They exist on the bare minimum. As it stands right now the minimum wage is somewhere between seven and eight dollars per hour. After a forty hour work week, the salary which a minimum hourly wage will provide is somewhere between $280 and $360. This is of course before taxes and is also with the exception of any random garnishment like let's say child support or something of that nature. Now let's examine what an individual is supposed to do with a check of this size, especially if this individual has a family. First there is paying rent. Let's say this person has a two bedroom. The going rate for a two bedroom in the city is about (and this is a real conservative estimate) about one thousand to fifteen hundred dollars per month. Now with that being said, it is pretty evident that that individual will not be living in the city unless it is in public housing. Now let's focus on that for a second. Living in public housing on a minimum wage salary will probably entitle the apartment dweller to about a two to three hundred per month rent. Now this is an absolutely great amount of rent to pay but look at potential downsides: the apartment will more than likely be in an unsavory area, which will more than likely be either plagued with drugs or crime or prostitution or all of the above. Now the second thing that this individual will more than likely be responsible for will be food. Now if this individual just has a child and no significant other, then a weekly allowance for food will probably be about one hundred dollars (unless of course this individual applies for and receives food stamps). The next thing an individual would have to spread his or her check over is something for him or her and the child to wear. Now when an individual considers the fact that a new pair of designer jeans for an adult can easily run over $60 and a designer shirt will be at least $30, the only feasible option that individual will have is to buy clothes from the goodwill or clothes off the clearance rack. Now mind you I didn't even include clothes for the child. Everybody knows that name brand sneakers for kids can easily run over one hundred dollars. Now what is a parent to do for a school age child who is trying to fit in, submit to the will of fashion and go broke or have their child be a laughing stock? Now we have covered the basic amenities such as rent, food and clothing. Now what's left in a semi modern home these days is entertainment. There is the playstation, xbox psp – you name it. The average child has to have at least one of these things to alleviate the stresses from daily school life and again, to not be laughed out of the cool group. In addition to all of this, there is the allowance that many children request or if not an allowance, then money to have to go to the store while they are out with friends. Now let's go back to the parent for a second; what if that parent wanted to possess a cell phone? The average cell phone bill is about $50 dollars per month unless of course you decide to opt for the free phones, which come along with an unmistakably cheap sounding ring tone as well as the clearance rack design. These phones are dependable (yes I've had one) but as far as the minute plan, don't try to have an extended conversation with anyone. Nowadays to watch television in your home, you need to have either cable or some service that you have to pay for. Now for all of you who have been paying attention, you will see that achieving the above is impossible. Wait, let me rephrase that. Achieving the above is impossible if you work a minimum wage job. But here's the real bullshit in this world – many of these employers have the nerve, the gall, the outright audacity to expect, rather demand that an employee be happy and thankful that he has a job of this sort. I remember the last minimum wage security job I had and life with it was just as I previously described. The supervisors used to become upset with me because I didn't smile. They would always berate me because I did not present myself as a happy and welcoming presence when posted in the lobby of some billion dollar corporate building. And this is one of the reasons why I moved from job to job so much. My thing was if I had to work forty hours a week and barely had any money by the middle of the week, what reason was there for me to smile? They used to tell me 'be happy, you have a job' or 'something is better than nothing' but that right there was nothing more than a prime example of more bullshit because I used to ask them 'would you do your job for my pay?' They barely had time to catch their breath in between all of the laughter. I used to agree with them that something is always better than nothing but when you can't pay your bills because you want to eat that is not better than nothing. That *is* the equivalent of nothing. This is what I believe to be little more than the powers that be having complete control over the working class. They know that the majority of people who want to live well will not be able to do so and that a good portion of them will resort to other tactics, some illegal, to facilitate their dream of good living. This will cause certain people to go to jail. This will cause more prisons to be built, thereby giving more jobs to people – so wait, maybe minimum wage is a good thing if in the end it will provide more employment? (For those of you who don't know, I'm being sarcastic now.) Minimum wage does little to help the average individual live a happy life. It forces you to live within your means. Nobody <u>wants</u> that. People <u>accept</u> that. People want the best in life. They do not want to settle for second best. Unfortunately when you work a minimum wage job that is exactly what you are doing. Even though I do not like the lottery, I am going to continue to play. And if by some ginormous stretch of luck, or divine intervention, I happen to win several million dollars, I will quickly work on achieving one of my dearest goals. One of the first purchases I plan to make is to seek out one of my former minimum wage jobs and purchase the company. Then I will switch the pay from most to least. And by this I mean that the asshole bosses and supervisors who laughed in my face when I would ask them if they would do their job for my pay, would have to do just that. I would give them the option of continuing to work for the company at their same position but with a minimum wage salary. And the ones who are presently making minimum wage will have a chance at seeing what it feels like to take home a paycheck that they can actually do something with. I would then wait in extreme anticipation to see which one of these laughing assholes would tell me some shit about how happy they are about having a job or something is better than nothing. Oooh! Come on mega millions jackpot, come to papa!

On Reality Shows

Reality shows, rather the idea behind many if them is that they are based on actual reality. **Here comes the bullshit:** They are not based on reality. These shows are nothing more than what I like to call logic deprivation entertainment and many of the people who watch them become so entwined with the lives of the characters and their families that they completely ignore the lives of their own. From about the last ten years or so, there have popped up reality shows of every type size and description. There have been shows about housewives from almost every state in the union. There have been shows about the wives of famous sports stars. There have been shows about fat people trying to lose weight. There have been shows about this state. There have been shows about that state. There have been shows about skinny people. There have even been shows about college kids, just to name a few. I have to give it to a lot of them – many of these shows are quite entertaining but that's it. There is little positive educational value contained within these reality shows. There is often little to be learned other than the fact that anybody can be a reality show star because that position requires little if any talent whatsoever. The entertaining part about these shows is not the intellectual part but the staged anger and hostility. Many people have argued me down talking about those fights are real and such but anybody with half an ounce of common sense knows that real fights will not be allowed on national television. Real fights or actual reality entails people getting hurt. Real fights entail people getting killed. Real reality is what you see when you look out your window. It is people getting shot over trivial things. It is little children getting run over by hit and run drivers. It is police officers doing illegal shit and constantly getting away with it. This is reality. This is the shit you don't see and why - it's because people in this world who love and can't stand to be without their favorite reality shows, cannot really tolerate reality. What this is, is what I like to call fantasy reality. I remember while growing up in the 70s & 80s, the meaning of the word housewife was an unemployed woman who took care of the home and family. This is all she did because this was all she had time to do. The societal roles were as such – the man went to work and the woman stayed home and made sure the house was taken care of. She was in essence married to the house, hence the term 'housewife.' Now according to these 'reality' shows, housewives are anything but. They are holding down their families. They have recording contracts and shit. They have personal assistants. They have fights with their best friends every couple of episodes. They have affairs. And they do all of this – all while looking glamorous. Like I said, bullshit. The cop reality shows are not immune from the bullshit status either. They, just like the other 'reality' shows are merely entertainment for the mindless or fodder for aspiring assholes – oops, I meant aspiring law enforcement. On these cop shows, what the average person who watches will get is a healthy dosage of positive and professional police tactics. In other words, exactly what the fuck they want you to get. They will not show you 'reality' which often entails law enforcement officers unfairly and usually without provocation assaulting individuals who have not even been arrested. They will not show you law enforcement officials taking the job personal – in other words going above and beyond what is legally allowed by the penal code just because someone may have pissed the law enforcement official off. They will not show the law enforcement officers being human – in other words reacting not how they were trained to react in the academy but acting the way any normal person would react to an overly stressful situation. They will only show you law enforcement performing at the optimal level of performance all the time. And you and I both know what this is – bullshit! Personally I have been assaulted by members of law enforcement and for little more than questioning the reasoning behind why I was being arrested. They don't show that shit on television, do they? Of course not. Reality shows are captivating. They are intriguing. They are even fun. But rarely are they true. The reason why I believe they are so successful is because people want to believe that this is what actual reality is. Reality is what you and I (the ones reading this book) experience on a day to day basis. It is not what the producers tell these actors and actresses to do when they are in front of a camera. When you are in front of a camera and you have to limit your activities to a half hour or hour or however long and you can only do what is allowed by 'law' then that is not actual reality. That is staged reality. That is fantasy reality. In short, that is fake or as I like to call it, bullshit!

84

On Employment

One of the best feelings in the world (besides sex ☺) is the feeling of being able to say 'I have a job.' Employment allows people to live better lives. It allows people to take care of their families and it allows them to do things they would otherwise not be able to do had they not been employed. **Here comes the bullshit:**

Why is it that the most important jobs in this world almost always seem to pay the least? I mean correct me if I'm wrong but shouldn't the financial disbursement of a job be commensurate to its importance? The care and protection of another person I believe is paramount. This is why I believe babysitters and caretakers of the elderly, as well as the security field and the police should be among the highest paid salaries. Don't get me wrong – I am not saying I am a fan of all of the above groups, especially police, I just believe fair is fair and right is right. The job description of these groups has got to be among the most important because if you really sit down and think about them individually, babysitters are entrusted with the care of human lives. Now granted they are not expected to heal or repair people's health when something goes awry, like say a doctor or a nurse. They are however expected to keep things from going wrong in between the visits to the doctors and nurses. Not on the same level but pretty damn close. This world basically trivializes the importance of certain types of care because if it didn't, the care behind a human life would certainly exceed that of minimum fucking wage. I haven't forgotten about teachers either. I do believe they should be included as one of the higher paid professions. After all they are laying the foundation for future society. The one thing about teachers I can't completely come to agreement with is their motives for doing what they do. I mean ask any underpaid, stressed out educator and almost every last one of them will tell you that they are not in it for the money. They will tell you that they are in it because they love the job. Pardon me for my opinion but I think that is a complete crock of shit. Granted, a person can actually love children to the point of overlooking the fact that the salary they receive for teaching those children is barely enough to commensurate the effort but one must take into account the fact that there are some bad ass fucking kids out here. Many people may get upset behind the previous statement and say things like kids are not bad, they are misguided and to an extent I believe that may be true but no amount of misguided 'ness' can explain kids assaulting teachers, disrespecting and or generally undermining the authority teachers have been endowed with. I can understand the loving and working with small children because for one, they are still impressionable and for the most part able to be molded into decent, law abiding human beings but once the foundation is laid and some of these children become animals, be it due to parental influence or parental neglect, I doubt if any amount of love for the job can supersede the necessity of cash! The truth, which many people want to try and deny, is money is paramount when it comes to why people choose the jobs they do. If it weren't, people would do their jobs for free. It is nothing more than an excessive amount of bullshit when individuals say they love their jobs more than the pay they receive and that is why they accept low salaries. Here's a for instance: Everybody knows they have volunteers in schools. Why can't one of these people who 'loves his or her job so much' complete all the required years of study to become an educator and then work in a school for free? The answer is simple. Everybody who wants to work for free, can't. Today's economy makes that pretty close to impossible. If a person did not need money, then I can completely understand them uttering the above statement about being in it for the love but for the most part, everybody I have ever met is not in a position to turn down any type of financial disbursement. People need money to live and as much as they would like to work for free, or as noble as the thought of working for free sounds to the average person, you work for free in this day and age, it's a pretty safe bet that you will soon be homeless. As for the caretakers of the elderly, for the most part, these people are a godsend. These people are put in place to make sure that elderly and homebound individuals who cannot adequately take care of themselves or who have no one to adequately take care of them are taken care of. I don't believe that these people chose this type of job for the pay it provides. I believe that they sincerely enjoy helping people live healthy and comfortable lives. For the pay they receive, (which is not that much) they could have worked many other menial jobs with a lot less recognition.

Focusing on the other two aforementioned professions, (security and police) it is extremely difficult to believe that people will endure much of the shit that is required for the sole reason of money. Security work, rather contract security work has long been hailed as one of the most hated, lowest paying, lowest respected jobs ever created. It is not a job that anyone with half an ounce of sense will say 'I can use this job to adequately take care of myself and family.' It is a job that people do while searching for better employment or it is a job people do because they have little to no education. I am not being harsh when I say this because I have worked in the security field for close to twenty years and I have seen more than my share of unqualified, unmotivated, un – whatever word you wanna use to fill in the blank with people in these types of positions. Many of these people are there because security companies will many times take just about anybody. And they will pay just about the lowest salaries that just about anybody will accept. Security should most definitely be among the higher paid careers because of the simple fact that security personnel are always or usually the first ones to be seen. They are in the line of fire so to speak because they have on these black or blue or whatever color uniforms which are often mistaken for law enforcement. Security is often the one who has to notify law enforcement and after law enforcement leaves, security is the one who has to deal with those that he or she has notified law enforcement about. Many contract security guards do not have weapons and are therefore in the face of danger everyday often trying to rather expected to do the job of law enforcement with about $1/10^{th}$ of law enforcements training. Some security personnel are expected to keep watch over millions of dollars worth of equipment or merchandise with nothing other than their wits, a bullshit eight and or sixteen hour training class, and possibly a walkie talkie. They are expected to play arbitrator, peacekeeper, authority figure, information and assistance provider, as well as protector. And all this for not much more than minimum wage. This is bullshit. Now I'm going to tell you about what I believe to be a gigantic, ginormous, gargantuan even, amount of bullshit when it comes to contract security. I have mentioned previously that I have been working in the field of security for almost twenty years. That's bad enough but that is not the bullshit of which I speak. One of the organizations, which contracted the company I worked for had a CEO who reportedly earned a net hourly salary, which was more than the annual salary of yours truly. So let me see if I can put this in laymen's terms for those who may not be able to understand. This motherfucker who is the president of the building I work in makes more in an hour than I do in a fucking year?! Let me see if can simplify this a little more. I can bust my ass coming to work everyday, putting up with people I don't like, vagrants who are often smelly and morally corrupt, as well as those who constantly disrespect my authority and after three hundred and sixty five consecutive days, I still will not have made as much as his punk ass does on a typical hour long lunch break? That is some real bullshit! Now granted it is in no way his or anybody else's fault that I decided to discontinue my schooling and get involved in this illustrious field of low fucking paying security, but when you look at the liability factor, the potential lawsuits that I and others like me who work for you are helping your organization craftily avoid, I'm sure you can easily see why I say that nine, ten, eleven or even twelve dollars an hour to do what we do is an extreme level of bullshit. Then people wanna go and wonder why some security guards don't smile. Why the fuck you think?

With police, it is pretty much the same as the other groups. They are entrusted with the care and protection of human lives and property but paid mere peanuts when you consider that they must put their lives on the line daily to do so. Now being a minority member from the big city, it is increasingly difficult to be an actual fan of the police department but I have to respect the job that they are hired to do. Knowing that people want to kill you just because of the job you have, or because they want to break the law and you are the only thing standing between them and that goal makes it increasingly difficult to believe that a person will do this job just for the money. If it were me I would expect rather demand that my pay scale be somewhere between eight to nine hundred thousand per year. Are you one of those people who feel that that is an excessive amount? Think about it, would you or any other sensible person actually risk your life and your family's security for what, 30 or 40k per year? I don't think so. That amount of pay for such a potential sacrifice is ludicrous. In other words, bullshit. Now granted, I am sure that there are a few twisted individuals who like to abuse the power that comes with being an officer of the law – and the fact that the position pays around 30 – 40k per year, that is little more than an added perk. But I do not believe that this is true for the majority of law enforcement personnel. I believe that most of them would more than likely agree with my rate of pay as being their starting salary. People accept jobs for the security, perks and benefits that those particular jobs provide but the bottom line is people work for money.

If you really want to know how much or how important your job is worth, don't do it – and watch the ramifications.

On Government Assistance Programs

These are bullshit, bullshit, bullshit! I'm sorry but due to my experiences and the experiences of many other individuals with certain agencies, I can think of no other way to start this chapter. There are many agencies put in place to help those of us who may need help during certain times of our lives. Some of those agencies are the social security administration, the human resource administration, Medicaid, Medicare and unemployment. Now I have been diligently trying to figure out which agency ranks the lowest among the ones listed here but I have been somewhat stumped because every time I seem to have a solid winner, a new facet of bullshit pops up. Let's start with unemployment. From my understanding, this 'help' was put in place so that individuals who were separated from their jobs would not go without some form of financial aid. By most accounts this would be a very noble gesture – man loses his job, give him some money until he finds himself a new job. This way, the man would not starve because he has no food. He would not go to jail because he has been caught stealing to provide for his family. He would not have to endure dirty looks from his significant other emanating from the silent thought of 'he's just a typical lazy ass man.' From most accounts, everything would be okay. **Now here comes the bullshit.** Unemployment only pays a person a percentage of what that person used to make at his job. If I'm not mistaken, the percentage is somewhere around thirty six. That means less than half. So let me see if I understand this correctly; a person works at a job which more than likely is only providing him enough money to barely make ends meet. That person gets fired or laid off or whatever and is expected to make ends meet with less than half of what he was bringing home before? That's beyond bullshit! If unemployment was a program where a person made exactly what he made while working, I would see little wrong with its existence. I mean of course time limits would have to be implemented, like they are now because there would always be the possibility of people getting spoiled by the continued flow of money for nothing. And a person would have to show up every so often to provide proof that he or she is diligently seeking new employment - like they also do now. An agency, which is supposed to help certain individuals, should actually help those individuals. Social security? I will only say two words, death benefit. The going rate for a funeral these days is somewhere around five grand with some discount retailers providing services for as little as three – yet the one time lump sum death benefit which social security so graciously gives is two hundred and fifty five bucks. Now using my somewhat limited computational skills, I figure this benefit to be about more or less, ten percent of the complete funeral cost. What does ten percent really get a person these days – alive or dead? If the total cost of the casket was three thousand, then a person would probably only be able to bury his legs – below the knees of course.

Next comes the human resource administration. The human resource administration or HRA is another name for welfare & food stamps. This agency is supposed to provide a benefit of cash and or food for individuals who are either unemployed or underemployed. And not meaning to take anything away from them because they do – it's just that the amount of benefit that they do give to people is not enough for anybody to actually live on. Let's take food stamps for example. For a single individual, the benefit is broken down to somewhere around forty bucks a week. Now let's break that down a little bit further. Seven days in a week. Seven into forty comes out to about five dollars and some change per day. When you consider that the average person eats out at least one meal everyday and the average price for take out is at least five dollars, that individual will be left with minimal funds to carry him throughout the month, especially if that individual attempts to eat more than one take out meal per day. Now I'm sure that the majority of you reading this or the majority of you who receive food stamps can attest to the level of bullshit there is in this policy but let's delve a little bit deeper into the bullshit pit and examine how these individuals at this agency actually come to arrive at the figure for their disbursement. The first thing these geniuses will do after requesting proof of address and identity is ask for proof of income. This is completely understandable because in order to combat the overwhelming amount of fraud in this country, certain preventative measures should and must be taken. So in order to make sure you are who you say you are and you make what you claim you make, they will ask for letters mailed to your home, such as rent statements, electric bills and at least four pay stubs from current employment. I agree with all of the aforementioned methods except the pay stub thing and here's why. Instead of basing their determination of eligibility on what you actually take home after taxes and deductions, these fools (and I'm not talking about those who work for these agencies but the system itself) will base your acceptance on the gross amount of your paycheck. Now here's the real bullshit: If you make ten dollars an hour or $400 a week but have to pay child support or some other wonderful deduction including taxes and are left with somewhere around $200 per week, these people will overlook that fact and use the $400 to either accept or deny your claim or think to themselves that since you're making so much, you should only need a little bit of help if any at all. Now I don't know anybody who can live comfortably on two hundred dollars a week. Remember I said comfortably. People do exist on this amount of money but most times they are miserable as shit. That's bullshit!

Now, before I get too far off the subject of food stamps, I have noticed some new bullshit about some of the regulations, which govern their use. They have this asinine rule, which states that food stamps can buy food for human consumption – as long as that food which is for human consumption is not hot. What kind of bullshit is that? What the food stamp agency is basically saying is that a hungry person can buy any and everything except a toasted bagel or a cheeseburger or just your ordinary run of the mill, hot sandwich. That's really messed up because if you really think about it, the only time they want you to have hot food is when you buy cold food and take it home and cook it. I mean that's not really so bad because many people who are on food stamps can cook their asses off but what about the rest of us? What happens when we get tired of eating cold sandwiches each and everyday? What about those people who do not possess even the most basic of marketable skills such as knowing how to cook? What are they supposed to do? Most people who fall into that category would resort to fast food establishments like Mc Donald's or Burger King and the like but here's the bullshit – food stamps are not accepted at fast food establishments and for two reasons. The first is that the food, which these places serve is hot and the second is that it is not served in a supermarket. Somebody please explain this to me; I mean although the food which these establishments serve may not be the utmost in beneficial health products, they do taste really good and it is able to be consumed. In almost every business, which accepts food stamps, there is a guide on what food stamps can and cannot buy. On this guide it clearly states that food stamps can buy items for human consumption. Approximately all of the people I've met I believe are human and the majority of them love to consume McDonald's and Burger King – so why can't we use food stamps to do so? I believe it's because whoever thought up the idea of food stamps, just like those other government assistance programs, wants all of those who receive it to be miserable. Here's my thing; if you're going to give someone money, give them enough so that they can live – not enough to have them continuously come back all the while complaining about how little they have to live on and how they can't make ends meet. If you're going to give someone food or the resources to acquire food, them give them enough so that they can adequately sustain themselves and their families without the worry of going hungry. I used to hear many people say that the system was designed for certain people to fail. I do not know if the certain people they were talking about were minorities or those who weren't affluent but think about something – when they give you money, it's never enough to live the way you want to. When they give you food stamps, it's never enough to eat the way you want to. When they give you unemployment, it's never enough to live the way you want to. My understanding of these assistance programs is that they give you just enough to keep you coming back. They give you enough just enough so that you can live the way they want you to live. They give you just enough so that you are under their control. That's some real bullshit ain't it?

On This Getting To Know Thing

When many relationships are contemplated or initiated, those involved often hold off on indulging in intimacies until they get to know the individual they are interested in a little better. This seems like or would seem like the best thing an individual could do, especially with the state of affairs regarding sexually transmitted diseases and the psychotic nature of certain individuals nowadays. People who hold off on relations are going so far as to do background checks regarding an individual's character, prison record, and even dating history. **Now here comes the bullshit:** There is no textbook timeframe period for getting to know somebody. The reason why I say this getting to know someone thing is bullshit is because how well a person deems knowing someone well enough is solely based on this person's own criteria. This means that if one individual says two weeks is all that's necessary to know someone before the sex is had and another person says that three days is a sufficient amount of time and still another says that the minimum waiting period is six months, then all three are correct. Getting to know someone has so many different levels of criteria that one may never know which criteria is being used to judge this person's worthiness when it comes to being a potential mate. For some people, getting to know someone entails only time – meaning as long as they are around this person on at least a semi occasional basis and for an unwritten specified amount of time, at the end of that time period, they will have gotten to know that person well enough. For some people, getting to know entails getting to know only this person's sexual history, meaning if the person they are interested in is a virgin, then they are automatically a good, rather great candidate to do the mattress mambo with. For some people getting to know entails meeting the family, interacting with the family and having the family confirm everything that the significant other has told the other about his or her life. These are all effective counter measures against deception but here's the thing that everybody and their mother and father should already know: Deception has no time limit! You can know somebody for a year or you can know somebody for ten years and still be tricked by deception. The more an individual knows about another, the less chance deception has to topple that person's relationship but note: deception can exist no matter how well one person knows another. In the case above where an individual will get to know the person they are interested in for several weeks or several months or whatever, the person that they think they are getting to know could just be showing the other exactly what the other wants to see. Some people lead a relationship without knowing it and some people just go along because it's easy as well as convenient. Granted an individual will never, let me say this again: an individual will never know everything about another person but it is highly recommended that an individual find out all he or she can about the individual he or she is planning to spend a portion of his or her life with. This goes for both parties. An individual can't be all knowing and secretive at the same time. People in relationships have to be open with one another to prevent future deception and heartache. In the case above where an individual bases the prospect of physical intimacy on just an individual's sexual history, they should be fully aware that **people fucking lie!** One of the biggest lies that people can concoct is the one about never being sexually involved with anyone. What do you honestly think will happen when some horny individual, who is otherwise careful or selective when trying to secure someone for a sexual rendezvous, hears the person he or she is interested in utter the 'I'm a virgin' line? He or she will almost assuredly drop all defenses and say JACKPOT! And then attempt to make the sexual experience the best the 'virgin' will ever have. This includes not always using the required protection. I mean there aren't many tests that an individual can use or that an individual will submit to, to prove that he or she is in fact a virgin but people have to use more than that one piece of criteria to deem someone worthy of sexual relations. When a lot of people hear the word 'virgin' how often do they say 'I need to give this person a STD test' as opposed to 'I'ma be the first one to rock his or her world!' I'm guessing not that often. A lot of folks may be surprised to hear this but a lot of other people would rather be someone's first than use common sense and look at that person the way everybody in this world should be looked at – carefully. Remember you don't know anybody in this world. You only know what they show and tell you.

In the case above of an individual getting to know the family of the person he or she is interested in, it should be adamantly stated again that people fucking lie. People in relationships lie. People contemplating relationships lie. People will even have their family members lie for them to procure a relationship. I know a lot of people will find this hard to believe but a parent will rarely say 'my daughter is crazy as shit' or 'my son likes to beat on women' even if they know that these things are true. They will many times add that ever so perfect layer of sugarcoating to the effect of 'my daughter has had a hard time finding a good man' or something to that effect. In the case of the wife beating son, most times, the family won't even bring that up. They will say anything to present their children and siblings in the best light possible and this is because they know that whenever the complete truth is told, it often makes for complete disaster. Think about something: if there was infidelity in each relationship that a son or daughter had and those relationships ended because of it, do you think the parent will divulge that information to the prospective partner? I seriously doubt it. Unless of course the parent likes the prospective partner more than they like their own son or daughter – and yes sometimes this happens. The reason I am telling you this is because I want people to realize that you cannot just rely on one piece of criteria and have it be the determining gauge for the entire relationship. It takes sometimes years and years to get to adequately know somebody and if you are in a relationship with this person, it may quite possibly take even longer. Getting to know somebody completely, especially somebody a person is in a relationship with after just a few short weeks or months is complete and utter bullshit.

On Common Law Marriages –

Somebody please introduce me to the genius who came up with this concept. Common law is the belief that if a couple stays together for a certain number of years without getting married in the traditional sense, then in the eyes of the law, almost as if by some miraculous and magical circumstance, that couple will be seen as married. Let me see if I can elaborate on this a little further – if a couple stays together for the specified amount of time, whatever that time may be, that couple will somehow be entitled to the same rights and benefits as a couple that has signed the marriage certificate and walked down the proverbial aisle? Let me see if I can elaborate on this a tad bit more; a husband that is married under the common law statute cannot acquire health insurance from his wife but if they were to break up after the specified time of common law marriage, the wife can get a big percentage of the husband's assets? That is some bullshit! I honestly believe that the whole idea behind common law marriage is so that women (and yes for the purpose of this point I am being a bit sexist) will be compensated for their time and for the trouble they have endured during their time in the relationship. I say women because when do you ever see a man attempting to acquire something tangible from his ex after the relationship is over – unless of course it specifically belongs to him? With this common law nonsense, women the world over are now given the ability and weaponry to hurt a man just because they feel or may feel that he has hurt them. If the idea behind common law marriages was one, which dealt with total equality, men would be able to ask for and be compensated for their time and turmoil in the relationship just like women. But we know this will never happen and here's the reason why; in relationships, whether they be boyfriend and girlfriend, common law marriages or regular marriages, men are supposed to, rather expected to break up without feeling. They are expected to possess the attitude of fuck you bitch, bye, sayonara and all that other good shit and the women are supposed to cry and beg the man not to leave. Men are always seen as stronger than women and women for the most part, are seen as weaker, always needing help from the man or just generally vulnerable.

Fortunately life is not always like that. Now, couples that do not get married for whatever reason don't need to worry. In the eyes of those that matter, the relationship will be considered enough of a 'marriage' so that all of the rules of an actual marriage apply. **Now here comes the bullshit:** This common law thing is only available in certain places. If you live in the United States, then this common law thing may be available to you in your state but it may not be available to your neighboring state. So (don't quote me on the actual states in which this common law thing applies but) a woman could be a wife in New York but nothing more than a girlfriend in New Jersey. That is some bullshit. And the people who believe in this common law thing should be able to clearly see that it is. If a couple were actually and legitimately married in one state, then common logic would dictate that that marriage would be recognized throughout every other state. See the difference? What this common law statute does is legitimize the practice of shacking up. Talk about the separation of church and state. The church dictates that premarital sex is wrong, so unless a couple is living together without having sex, they are violating the laws of Christianity. The state dictates that if you violate the laws of the church long enough, as what common law pretty much is, we will reward you for doing so. Ain't that something?

Some will rationalize that this common law thing is nothing more, rather little more than an unnecessary label. It is like the father's day and mother's day and even secretaries day thing. All of these days are invented to give acknowledgement and appreciation to the above stated groups and more but here's the bullshit: why is it only on one day or during one week are people supposed to show appreciation and acknowledgement? That stipulation right there makes the entire effort seem fake. Here's an example: If a person does not have money on mother's or father's day to purchase and send a card or gift to his or her parents, does that mean that he or she loves them any less than someone who sends a bouquet of roses or a bounty of cash on those particular days? Of course not. But this is the perception that many ignorant people have and why, it's because people the world over have been brainwashed to believe that if a person does not do what everybody else is pressured to do, then that person is somehow less than honorable or desirable than the others who have followed the crowd. Getting back to common law, it is something, which in my opinion, is not meant to be taken seriously. I believe it is another method of pacification for women who are not getting married by their lovers, boyfriends and fiancées. It is little more than a removable title, which is given to couples so that some snippet of importance or significance can be given to their otherwise teenage relationship resembling union. Common law is not respected by everyone and in my opinion until it is, it should not be respected or accepted by anyone. But that's just my opinion.

On This Lottery Thing

Let me be the first to say it; the idea behind the lottery is a wonderful thing! The chance to actually become a millionaire with only one dollar is absolute genius! This would be the most perfect idea in the world if it weren't for the fact that it is a complete and utter crock of **bullshit!** Here's why I believe this is so: Listening to what seems like an endless monologue about our nation's crippling debt crisis makes me compulsively wonder, how in the fuck can the lottery commission or whoever the fuck it is that is responsible for the payouts of these lottery winnings afford to give one, two and even three hundred million dollar payouts every so often when there is seemingly no money anywhere else in this damned country? I have played the local lottery for a few years. I have even traveled to different states to play the Powerball lottery when they were not available in my home state. I don't think I have ever won more than a hundred dollars. With that being said, how is it that there's the ability to give an individual or group upwards of three hundred million dollars just because this lucky motherfucker invested a dollar? Can you understand my concern? This is the same as one person going up to another and saying 'I will give you a one dollar bill and you will give me three hundred million dollar bills back.' I just don't think that shit is right – especially with all the homelessness and poverty in this country. This is supposed to be the richest nation on earth. So then how does this happen? If they and by they I am referring to those who run the lottery, are able to give away at least one hundred million every so often, shouldn't they be able to help, rather significantly help with the debt?

Forgive me for my sometimes and somewhat outrageous thought process but I think and this is just my personal belief that if you work for twenty or thirty years, putting up with people's shit, putting up with people's foul attitudes and just generally making yourself available to their nonsense, you should be awarded a million dollars – not some lucky son of a bitch who more than likely doesn't need it. Think about it; is it fair that somebody works their entire lives to get a bullshit ass pension so that they can live like a peasant while some dumb dick motherfucker who invests a dollar gets to live like a king? I don't think so. What I think is that the top lottery prize should be one million dollars. I do not believe that there is anybody who would disagree that one million bucks is a substantial amount of money and I also do not believe that there is anyone who would not be ecstatic about winning the million dollar prize – unless of course that person is already a millionaire or above. So here's my thing: if the lottery was to have a top prize of one million dollars, then the one, two and three hundred million extra dollars, that would have been used to pay a single entity or maybe even a group of people who decided to chip in to an office pool, could be used for the out of control debt or things of that nature. Let's go out on a limb here and say that those extra hundred millions could be used to put an end or at least a significant dent toward ending the scourge of homelessness in this country. Think about this; wouldn't it be great not having to see people exploit the homeless by taking pictures of them on the trains and just out and about and then posting those pictures on any random website for nothing more than their random entertainment? And wouldn't it also be great if tourists did not come over here from wherever it is they just happen to emanate from and take pictures of the homeless like they are a fucking tourist attraction? Wouldn't it be fucking great if people would not have to cover their noses every time a homeless individual enters a train car in anticipation of the raunchy smell which is usually associated with homeless people? Think about all of the jobs, which could be created with those seemingly endless supplies of mega million dollar jackpots. The problem with this country is that things have been made too easy for some folks. Win the lottery, never have to work again – and neither will your kids or their kids. This is a nice dream but wouldn't the lottery be better served if it was an entity, which helped people live better as opposed to allowing people to live stupidly. This is not an insult to any particular individual who may have already won the lottery but we have many times seen what some people do with their winnings, which can be described in no other feasible term but stupid. Some people win 100 million dollars then all of a sudden they have to go out and buy a 10 million dollar house. In addition to that, they then have to buy a million dollar car or two. And still in addition to that, they have to make everybody in their families and everybody that they consider a friend, rich as well. Then what happens? In a few years, the lottery winner is broke. Now granted some people, many people in fact don't like their jobs and at the first sign of a chance to get out, these people, me included, would jump ship and not look back but giving an individual all that money so that they forget what work, rather hard work is, is not the best idea. Most people, I would assume, do not plan for a lottery win, which is why many of them either end up hiring others to oversee their finances for them or they go broke. When people are forced to live according to budgeting a weekly or by weekly check and then all of a sudden are given the resources, which will basically make budgeting non existent, what realistically does one think is going to happen? They will blow that money on foolish things. Maybe and this is purely speculation here, about one in one million people would continue to pay their bills the way they have been paying them after a lottery win. Most people would take the impulsive route and completely pay off every bill they could find while at the same time creating new brand new and quite possibly, more expensive ones. You would almost never see somebody with the mindset of 'nothing in my life will change – I will continue to pay bills just the way I have been doing. I will continue to live just the way I have been doing. I will do everything as I ever have, only with a few million on standby just for emergencies.' From my experience and understanding, most people just want a little help. They do not want to be excessively rich. They do not want to be filthy rich either. They want to be able to not have to worry about bills. They want to be able to help their family members out of a tough financial jam. They want to pay for their kids schooling but they do not want to be billionaires. And this is why I believe a million dollar payout would be an excellent amount to satisfy most individuals. Think about something: a million dollars will not make anybody filthy rich. What it will do is provide enough so that people can be comfortable. It will give people the <u>option</u> of working or retiring. Now think about something else: many people make $25, 000 and under per year. Going with $25,000 as an example, an individual would have to work ten years to make $250,000, which is ¼ of one million dollars. This means that to amass one million dollars, that individual would have to work 4x as long. In other words, that individual would have to work for forty years. Now here's the thing; most people usually only plan on working twenty years, maybe twenty five and then retiring. Most jobs dictate that an employee works a minimum of twenty years before they are eligible for retirement. Who in the hell wants to work double that? Not me. Now here's the other thing: most of these people who work twenty plus years do not even make one million dollars. That's some bullshit ain't it? Now here's still another thing: if a person does work for forty years at the above rate of pay, that person will have made one million dollars. That person would not have one million dollars to spend; he or she would have just made one million dollars in total. Now if that person were to subtract all of his or her expenses during those forty years to include paying rent, raising kids, education, food and any other related expenses which just go along with daily living, that person probably would not even realize that he or she has attained the million dollar mark. This is why I believe the million dollar payout thing is a good thing. When you give people an exorbitant amount of money and the people who receive it have no conceptual idea of what to do with it, you are not creating a happy individual; you are more than likely creating an asshole.

In addition to the above nonsense, there is this thing going on nowadays about lottery pools, where groups of friends pool their money together in the hopes that if they were to claim the winning ticket, they would be able to split the money equally, still remain good, close friends and life as they know it would be wonderful. Okay – that right there is some bullshit. Here's proof: The day I am writing this section is a couple of days after one of the winners of the biggest lottery jackpot in history revealed herself. The jackpot was over half a billion dollars. Now this amount of money for a lottery jackpot is bullshit itself but what is even more bullshit is how the friends who entered the pool didn't act too friendly after the winner came forward and said that she had won by herself. Now this wasn't the first time this happened. There was another lottery pool where the winner said that he had the only winning ticket and what happened? The friends again did not congratulate him, they did not wish him the best, they took him to court and why? Because they did not believe that he purchased the ticket on his own. According to published reports, at least one of these lottery winners faced death threats because they would not share the money. This is not what's supposed to happen in a lottery pool. People are supposed to be happy that one of their friends or co workers won. But see here's the bullshit about the lottery and about people; people play with hopes, dreams and aspirations of never working again. They play in the hopes of being able to purchase every materialistic thing that their little hearts and feeble minds can fathom. They do not want to hear any bullshit about happiness for their fellow man or woman. They want what is theirs, even if it's not. See what money, rather the thought of money does to people? Personally, I would love to win the lottery but I would hate to have to fear for my life for doing so. Some people debate me when I say that the people who enter into these office lottery pools and such do it because of the pursuit of lifelong eradication of bills and the ability to do anything that they have ever envisioned but to those that do, I wish you could riddle me this – if the lottery winner were to give back the five, ten, fifteen or even twenty dollars which the losers in the pool invested, would that make everything alright? I think not. Wait, scratch the political correctness, hell fucking no, it wouldn't make anything right. It would make them mad as shit!

On This Retirement Thing –

Retirement is defined as the period of one's life after leaving one's job and ceasing to work. Retirement benefits are supposed to pay enough for the person who has retired to live comfortably until that person's death. Those benefits are supposed to allow older folks to enjoy their golden years. They are supposed to allow older folks to take cruises, take vacations, go to the casino and blow their entire retirement check on those one armed bandits, all the while cursing out any random author who attempts to take one of the two chairs they are simultaneously using to play those slot machines. **Now here comes the bullshit:** Many retirees are going back to work. This means that many folks in their sixties and seventies are going back to work and many more are out looking for work. Much of the blame is placed on our economy but I think a lot of the fault should be shouldered by those individuals who are forced to work. Many, maybe even most of the problems in this world start in the beginning of things. Problems in relationships quite often start because the parties involved either ignore little things in the beginning of relationships, which resurface later and cause detriment or they overlook things, which may become problems later on in the relationship. If people nip things in the bud, they will rarely if ever have a chance to blossom and cause problems later. Simple solution. Looking at this from a work standpoint, many people work paycheck to paycheck jobs. This means that if heaven forbid they lose their jobs one day, the next week they will be fucked. Now I am not making any kind of judgments here because I have done it. In fact as I type this line, I am doing it. I am just saying that if I, as well as many of the paycheck to paycheck working individuals had initially chosen a job with a better salary or a better retirement plan or even a 401k, maybe we would not be victims of this retirement bullshit that has been put in place for many of us to suffer through. Of course there is the thing of we all should have gone off to college and secured a great paying job – but here's the thing: everybody is not college material. Everybody does not have the two or four years required to secure a better salary and subsequently a better position in life. Some people have to work straight out of high school because they have either their own child or children to support or they have to care for siblings. Sometimes these people have to get jobs quickly because their parents are not the optimal figures in money management and they have to help keep the home from being foreclosed.

Here's where the bullshit starts to get deep: people work for let's say twenty or maybe thirty years until either voluntary or mandatory retirement kicks in. Let's hypothetically also say that one of these people makes a salary of about $50 per hour. Most retirement plans that I have heard of would offer this individual half of the highest salary this individual has made. My thing is if you have worked all of these years to attain that level of pay and have more than likely become accustomed to that level of pay, how can any reasonable entity expect you to live just as comfortable on half of that pay just because you are not working anymore? That's some bullshit. My idea of retirement is whatever pay you get while you're working should be the same amount of pay you get once you stop. Fuck a gold watch. I think everybody in the world would love to sit back and get paid for doing nothing. But this is not how the retirement system is designed. People work all these years only to receive an amount of money, which is nowhere near enough to allow these people to get what it is they worked for all of these years in the first place. How many jobs give a retirement package, which includes a boat? Not many. That's what I want. But my miniscule paying security job will never facilitate that. I don't even know if this job has a retirement package. It probably doesn't and why, it's because most of the individuals who get jobs in security either quit, die, get fired or wait, did I say quit? That's why I write these books. It's so that I can have the option of working – or not. It's so that I can sit back and not only watch but laugh my ass off at other people who decided to work for somebody they hated up until the day they received a bullshit ass pension or until the day of their deaths. It's so that I do not have to look like I am retired when I am. I want to look like an old cool dude with a young – scratch that – very young girlfriend. (Twenty two year olds are looking kinda good these days! ☺) I do not want to look the way most retirement plans force an individual to look. You know the look - the orthopedic shoes, the shorts pulled up to your chest, the ninety nine cent shirts, etc. Nobody wants to live like that. What kind of fucking existence is that? I will tell you. It is a pitiful, peasant like existence. People say that they are blessed and happy to be alive at that age but are they really? People say they don't need money at that age, just their health. I agree with the part that health is paramount when it comes to importance but how much fun is health when you can't do anything with it but stare out your window. How much is it worth when you have to depend on the bullshit social security and other programs they give you to sustain yourself? My thing is if you can't live happy, then why fucking live? Here's an idea for a retirement plan; why not instead of giving an individual half of his last salary after he retires or even his full pay for a retirement, give that individual double whatever his pay was when he reached retirement age? I'm pretty sure if more companies would enact this plan, a high turnover rate would be virtually non existent. Think about it; wouldn't that be an appropriate disbursement for someone who has worked faithfully for another for twenty or more years? I think so. Retirement is supposed to be a time of no more working. It is supposed to be a time of now I can do whatever it is I want to do. But when most people who have worked for another or for some city agency or some bullshit ass job for so many years, take an honest look at the money they have to sustain themselves throughout the rest of their years, they most often realize that they can't do shit. Some of them <u>have</u> to work after mandatory retirement because the money they receive is more or less like the minimum wage of today, a fucking joke. What I really think retirement should be called is hiatus-ment, because in certain situations, that's really what it is. A person is just on hiatus until he or she finds either a new job or a new source of income to help them live through their golden years. If you think about it, one would have to ask what is a person supposed to do when they reach retirement age and they are forced to live on half of their pay? If they have an apartment, which is not rent stabilized, how are they going to afford to continue living there? Chances are they will be forced to move out and become dependant on social services, end up living in either a residence for seniors or with relatives or friends. And there's a pretty good chance that they're going to be miserable while doing so. In my opinion, this whole system is wrong – from the just above minimum wage jobs to working all your life to provide for your family and then once you stop working, you have to be dependant on someone else to provide for you. This whole system is bullshit. With the retirement system the way it is, most of the working people will never experience true happiness and as mentioned before, if a person cannot live happy, then why fucking live?

On Rehab Clinics –

From my understanding, a rehab clinic is a place for people who are either injured or presently or previously on drugs or some kind of negative behavior to get well. Hence the term 'rehabilitation.' **Here comes the bullshit:** There are many rehab facilities, which allow treatment ranging from several weeks to several months and longer. That made me wonder. If a person has been on drugs for most of his or her life, then realistically how in the hell can that person get off drugs by going to rehab for several weeks or for several months?

This is some real bullshit – I mean how can a person be on drugs for a good portion of their life and then go to rehab for 30 or sixty days and then not be on drugs anymore? I believe that if a person smoked crack for ten years, for instance, then that person should remain in rehab for at least ten years to counteract the effects of that drug. The problem with many of these rehab programs today is that they offer just enough time for the person who is on drugs to miss the drugs. You know how absence makes the heart grow fonder? This is basically the same principle. If a person is separated from something they like, love or have an affection for, that person will eventually have a longing for it. If that person is kept away from that thing for an extended amount of time, then that person will eventually forget about it or replace it with something else. I have seen so many so called extreme drug addicts go to rehab clinics for a month or two, come home about twenty pounds heavier, stay clean for about a month and then its right back on to whatever it was they went to the rehab clinic to get off of. I went to one of these places – for about a day and one of the first things they tell you to do is to make a commitment to stop doing whatever it is you are doing which caused you to go there. I always and still do think that that is some counterproductive bullshit. I mean if an individual could actually tell himself to stop indulging in the negative behavior which would cause him to seek out a rehabilitation facility as a potential option in the first place, would that person actually need to ever even go to that rehabilitation facility at all? Kinda makes you say hmmm, doesn't it?

On This Whole Fidelity Thing –

When most people come together to form a relationship, more often than not, the belief or expectation of fidelity to one another comes along as well. **Now here comes the bullshit:** There is a ginormous amount of misconceptions floating about regarding what fidelity actually is. One of the biggest misconceptions of fidelity is the fact that it is often assumed and by assumed, I mean that if one person in the relationship shows fidelity to the other, then the same amount of fidelity is automatically reciprocated to the other. One of the definitions of fidelity is faithfulness to a person, cause or belief, demonstrated by continuing loyalty and support. Another definition is sexual faithfulness to a partner. Both of these definitions have the word faithfulness in the meaning and one meaning has the word continuing. Continuing is another word for constant. Nothing in this world is constant except change. The main reason why I think fidelity is bullshit is because of the fact that no one can accurately predict just how long it will last. Just like with the idea behind many relationships, people are under the mistaken impression that fidelity begins at the onset of a couple's union and automatically continues until the demise of that couple's relationship. I speak to people who have been on the receiving end of an affair almost all of the time and one of the first things they tell me they did to handle the hurt was to go out and have an affair of their very own. My thing is why would a person need to do that unless they had put more faith, trust and fidelity into that person than what was humanly possible or feasible. What many people in this year of 2012 still have not come to the realization of is the fact that <u>all</u> humans are capable of failure. This is proof that people make fidelity commitments to the wrong entity. If people were to make a commitment to a higher power or at least a commitment to being honest to one another, then maybe all of this infidelity would not be going on. In fact, I can almost guarantee that all of this infidelity would not be going on. If people did make fidelity commitments to the Man above and followed his law, whenever the significant other failed at fidelity and cheated, the other party would be able to say something to the effect of 'I will hold on to my faith.' 'I will remain steadfast.' 'I will not even worry about possible or actual transgressions because I know that he or she not only can fail but will fail.' 'It is not a matter of if he or she will falter but when.' If people just said I'm going to stay true to my higher power, there would be no urge for revenge and consequently no reason to cheat. But people don't do that. People look for the good in relationships and not only do they look for the good, they look for it so hard that they are willing to <u>completely</u> throw away common sense while trying to find it. Think about something; it is often said that around fifty percent (50%) of marriages fail or end in divorce. Yet people continue to jump into relationships at any and every chance they have. I guess they think that they will beat the odds or maybe that the odds don't apply to them. Whatever the case, those are not odds that any halfway intelligent individual would use to gamble their happiness on. Let's look at this from another angle, shall we? If it was common knowledge and not only common knowledge but a proven fact that fifty percent (that's half) of all aircraft that were to take off from any given airport were going to crash, nobody in their right fucking mind would take them. I damn sure wouldn't. And nobody that I can think of would take them either. So then why is it that people still jump into relationships the way they do? I guess this type of mathematical equation only applies to everything other than relationships or maybe people think that their relationships are going to defy all history as well as all logical reasoning. A lot of things in this world are done on impulse and many of those things are widely accepted such as shopping or even decisions regarding work situations. But when people jump into a relationship because of an impulsive urging, it then becomes one of the most idiotic things that people can do. An intelligent decision involves taking time. An impulsive decision involves taking risk. When an individual makes an impulsive decision regarding a relationship, he or she is not taking the time to find out if the one they are interested in is a good prospect for fidelity. These people are jumping into the relationship with little more than positive hope that the relationship goes well. This is not what should be done in regard to a relationship. This is what is called a gamble. This is what people do in casinos. The thing about people who gamble in casinos is that most of the time they lose.

I have noticed that many people get married in the sight of their higher power, in other words, before God. These people recite everything that needs to be recited during the ceremony to make everyone around believe that they actually believe in what it is they are saying. One of the things that always sticks out as an extreme level of bullshit is the part about loving and honoring the significant other. I call it bullshit because if there were actually all of this love and honor, would there be all of this infidelity? Which brings me to my next point: when it comes to fidelity, why is it that when someone in a relationship cheats on the other, the other immediately wants to go and exact revenge? Why can't they just say since marriage is a law of my higher power, I will sit back and let Him exact revenge? No, people don't do that. People say forget all that jaborwocky about religion and spirituality and all that good stuff – you hurt me, I am going to hurt you.

A while back, a friend confided in me that the relationship between him and his wife was ending. He told me that his occupation was the cause of his relationship ending. He was an out of state truck driver. He reasoned that the long hours and days away from his wife was what led her to stray. I really hope that my friend does not read this or if he does read this I hope that he does not take offense to my interpretation of his situation but the long hours away from one another was not the reason why the wife decided to cheat. She decided to cheat because she was a hoe (whore for you politically correct individuals). When people in relationships are away from one another, the absence is believed to make the heart grow fonder. In other words, the fact that the couple is apart will create a longing for the couple's reuniting. Because a person does not have continual and unrestricted access to sex does not mean that the only other option available is that of seeking out someone else to fulfill that desire. That excuse is a cop out. That excuse is bullshit. Cheating is a conscious decision. It is a decision, which is made by those who either do not have the strength to remain faithful or by those who have no intention on remaining faithful. Someone cannot make you cheat. This is what's meant by a conscious decision. Now a lot of people have tried to argue me down about a person not having strength but here's the thing – strength is not a birthright. It has to be taught and this goes for physical and moral strengths. Not everybody cheats when they and their partners are not having sex every other day. Some people pray for the strength needed to alleviate those sexual desires. Now I know what many folks are gonna say. They are going to say that not everybody uses prayer as a remedy for their problems – and I agree totally but here's the other thing: Not everybody just goes and hops on the first dick that comes along just because their husband is outta town either. The problem with many people is that they all want to believe that fidelity starts with the other person in the relationship at the same time it starts with them. They also want to believe that fidelity will last with the other person as long as it lasts with them. Now this is a wonderful sentiment and a wonderful starting point in relationships but when most relationships start, there is usually little to no adversity to test the strength and resilience of the relationship. What there is almost always an abundance of is 'I hope the happiness and new relationship euphoria that I'm presently experiencing will continue all throughout the relationship.' In other words, when people experience only good times during their relationships and base the continuance of the relationship on those good times, what ends up happening is the first bout of adversity is usually the last. What makes a relationship strong is not the way in which couples avoid adversity but how they conquer and get past adversity. Fidelity is not guaranteed in any relationship although it is heavily desired in most. What I believe this woman could have done besides praying for the strength to remove the sexual demons was communicate to her husband her feelings about the toll the job was taking on their relationship. She could have recommended – rather insisted that he accept a local route, which would have him home every night or every other night. I'm sure the husband would have willingly agreed – especially if he saw that the job was causing detriment to his relationship. But here's the thing; aside from the fact that fidelity is only a dream in many relationships, the communication that needs to be there, usually isn't. This is what causes problems when it comes to fidelity. People in relationships always think that they know what their partners desire and are in need of – and for some magical reason or another, they feel they know these things without ever having to discuss them with the significant other. These people feel that what fidelity means to one it automatically means to the other. Assumptions such as these are wrong but more than that they are dangerous. If a person in a relationship believes that cheating is engaging in sexual intercourse and the other believes that cheating is just spending time with a member of the opposite sex without the knowledge of the significant other, it is possible that a relationship or even a life may end because of a misconception.

On The Perceptions Of Black And White

It is extremely sad to say but in this year of 2012, stereotypes about certain races are still prevalent and not only are they prevalent, they are accepted and believed without question. The perceptions of black and white differ according to many factors. One of those is gender. For an example, one of the perceptions about blacks, rather male blacks when it comes to children is that the majority of them do not want to care for their children, whereas the women desire to have as many as possible. Is this perception always true? Of course not. But it is one, which many outside of the black community attach to people of color. For an example on the opposite side of the gender spectrum, it is much believed that all black women have what's known as the black woman's attitude. This is the 'oh no you didn't' thing where black women instantly transform into mega bitch whenever they are or feel that they are disrespected. Again, is this true? Of course not but it is how many of those outside of the black community and or race feel adequately define black people. Now in regards to the above, I like to believe that all men have a natural desire to be in the lives of their children but circumstances often make that desire impossible. Some of those circumstances include the fact that the mother of the child does not want the father to be in the child's life, for whatever twisted reason she could have. Another circumstance could be that the father is not financially stable enough to contribute adequately to the upbringing of the child. Think about it; if a man does not have any income, how will he be able to be a good father to that child? Love without liquidity can only go so far. In regard to the attitude thing attributed to black women, I like to believe that any woman who is or who feels disrespected will have the ability to instantly transform into mega bitch to let the disrespecting party know not to ever do that shit again. Does this mean over reacting? Sometimes. Maybe. Now do some black women over react? Of course they do, but I believe that over reactions occur in every race in existence. It's just that for some reason or other, black women are the ones given the credit for losing their damned minds. Let's take Ms. Lorena Bobitt for instance. I may be wrong here but I think that was the epitome of over reacting. And note; she wasn't black.

What follows are eight terms, which are commonly thrown around when relating to certain individuals.

Ghetto	Suburb
Under Privileged	Privileged
Not as educated	Educated
Violent	Passive

The above chart outlines two particular races, black & white. Although they are not specifically labeled, it is a pretty easy guess for most people who the above descriptions are attributed to. **Now here comes the bullshit:** The above chart does not in any way only apply to either race. There are both, black and white individuals who fall into each category. But it's the perceptions of society, which dictate that the majority of black people either live in, have lived in or know somebody who is in the ghetto. And it's those same perceptions of society that deem many white people as living in affluent areas like the suburbs. The thing about the term ghetto is that it not only encompasses a particular area. It also defines an attitude. It used to describe slum areas, which were overrun by minorities who dressed a certain way because they either knew no better or because they could not afford to do any better. Nowadays the ghetto seems to be something that people who normally would never step foot in are trying to emulate. Now it's not hard to find non minorities dressing the way people who are from the ghetto dress. Now it's not hard to find people who are not from the ghetto talking like they are, with the broken English, Ebonics and all types of slang. When people think of those that live in the suburbs, the perception almost automatically veers to the side of white people and this is because historically black people were not known or expected to reside in nice areas. It is why even until this day when a person notices a black person living in a historically or predominately white area or when a white person resides in a historically or predominately black area, the belief will be that the black person is rich or married to a white person or the white person is poor or if not poor, then not as affluent as those who could afford to live in predominately white areas.

122

Continuing with the bullshit list above, the belief is quite extensive that blacks are under privileged and white people are quite the opposite because of the pigmentation thing. There is even the affirmative action thing, which I think is based on that fact. Now I won't get into whether or not I think the 'action' thing is right or fair but I will say that the belief of blacks being under privileged just because they are black is some bullshit. Personally, I believe that that perception has a great deal to do with education. I also believe that everybody starts out in life pretty much the same. Now it is very true that many people who fall into the category of disadvantaged just happen to be black but this is not always because of drug and alcohol abuse as many would like to believe. It is also not because of black people being any less intelligent than their white counterparts. Many times the opportunity to advance one's education is not there at the same time it is for other races. Many times black people have siblings who need to be taken care of which causes education to be put on the back burner. Sometimes education is frowned upon during different stages of an individual's life as opposed to having fun. Many times certain black people focus on sex before education, whereas many whites do the opposite. This might explain why there are so many minority parents going to school later in life to attain their degrees after their children are off on their own as opposed to many non minorities who wait until after they finish their schooling to have kids.

Now it is true that some parents of black children are preparing them for an uneducated classification in life by letting the schools and the television network producers educate them but does this mean that black people are any less able to learn than other races? Of course not. Some of these parents do not focus on education the way it should be focused on. They believe that the school system will provide all that is necessary for a proper and productive upbringing – and in some cases this is believed to be appropriate but schools are only part of the equation. It is the parent's job to make sure that the children are taught right. Schools are put in place to either pass or fail. They are not here to make to make sure that an individual learns. That is the responsibility of a parent. Look at the difference – parenting is for life. School is for as long as you want it. If a school does not maintain a record of passing students, the school will close. If a parent doesn't teach a child, that child will just not learn from the parent. Now here's where the money thing comes into play. If Ivy league educators were to work for free in inner city schools with disadvantaged students as diligently as they do in privileged areas with affluent students, would there be any difference in the level of information which is retained? I think not. I think you get what you pay for. I think if you pay for a teacher with average grades to teach kids, then those kids will learn average lessons. If you have top of the line teachers teaching every child that attends an educational institution, whether it be Harvard or P.S. 67, all kids would receive a top of the line education and there would be none of this bullshit about black not being as smart as white or vice versa.

If people can't afford to go to certain institutions, their true educational value or level will more than likely go undetermined or unappreciated

A lot of people have this perception or misconception or general belief that many black folks are not as smart as other races. My question is 'where does this belief come from?' I used to think that it was because of the preponderance of black folks in jail but then I did some research and found that blacks are disproportionally incarcerated more than whites but are a smaller percentage than whites. This means that if there were a town of 100 people, half being black, more than half would be in jail. Now there is a good reason why this happens. I believe it's because a lot of times, police are assholes. Now don't get me wrong but I have seen police go on hunting missions for black folks like black folks have nothing else to do but spend time in jail. Elsewhere in this book I speak about why I believe the police and related law enforcement officials are excuse the term, full of shit. But this is not why I believe the perception of uneducated black people exists. Think about something; if back people were really as unintelligent as others make them out to be, would there be any black billionaires? I mean I do understand that there are a disproportionately smaller amount of them as compared to other races but there are some. If black folks weren't that smart, would there even be one? Of course not. But people have become so brainwashed by society's perception of inner city and low income black folks that they are often unable to extricate themselves from that particular way of thinking when it comes to people who do not live in the inner city or who are classified as low income. And here's the bad thing; many black people help this perception of un education along by living the way they do. Many black people can go to school and get degrees but yet they choose to sell drugs. Many black people can work yet they choose to steal. Now just like above, these things are not only perpetrated by black people. Both black and white people sell drugs and steal in lieu of working and or going to school. Black people however just seem to get most of the credit. Some people believe that the reason for this perception started way back in the times of slavery and they believe this because they reason if black people were so smart, how could they become slaves in the first place? Is this a correct assumption? I think not but this is how some people think and reason. There are going to be perceptions such as this until the end of time. The fact that they exist does not make them right. The fact that some black people help perpetuate the stereotypes which lead to these perceptions do not make them right either.

When it comes to this thing about violence, there is so much of it from inner city neighborhoods to main street America, that to put a number on which race perpetrates it more is close to impossible. People are quick to say that black people are violent and white people for the most part are passive. I believe this to be a case by case basis. I know black people who run from violence as well as those who commit violent acts. I have also known white people to assault others and without much provocation. And the sad but true fact is that many of the people who get their information on just how bad other people are usually get that information from television. This is bad because it is unreliable. Not everyone who commits a violent act ends up on Cops or America's Most Wanted. Sometimes people both black and white commit unspeakable acts and are never prosecuted because of the fear they instill into their victims or because they have been lucky enough not to get caught. Color perceptions are wrong just like those according to gender but they are allowed to exist because of a lack of education. When people are presented with certain facts, they will believe them whether they are true or not and whether they are researched or not. A case, which is causing a great deal of turmoil and controversy, is the one involving Trayvon Martin. In case there is anybody in earshot of any media outlet who hasn't heard about this, it is the case of a Florida teenager who was shot by an individual who was supposedly protecting his neighborhood. The main reasons why this case has caused so much controversy is because for one, the young man, Mr. Martin was unarmed when he was gunned down, number two, the young man was black and number three, the individual who allegedly shot him wasn't. Now at the time of this book's printing, there is much speculation about what actually happened but there is even more speculation about why. Many people are asking would this have happened if Mr. Martin were white. Many people are asking would the alleged shooter be free at this present moment if he were black. Many people are asking if race played a part in this situation at all. Personally I think race played the biggest part in this situation but I wasn't there and I don't know the facts. Only God and the shooter do. I hope that the truth comes out soon and if it is a situation of race being an issue in why this young man lost his life then I hope the shooter finds himself in the warmest part of hell. Many people say that the hood that Mr. Martin wore contributed to his murder. I disagree with that opinion. I believe that the perception difference between black people and others who are not black is what was a ginormous contributing factor. The sad part is that when white people put on hoods, they are perceived as white people wearing hoods (unless of course that hood is accompanied by an all white outfit). When black people put on hoods, more often than not, they are perceived as something negative. Is it right? Of course not but it is a sad fact of life that the color of one's skin often dictates how other's judge and perceive them. And if an individual just happens to fall under the darker side of the spectrum, that person will be judged more harshly than not. This is probably the worst example of the perception difference between black and white but it is definitely a true example of how society still views certain races in the year of 2012. I know this is a futile wish but this shit really needs to change.

Getting back to some of the other perception differences between black and white, white people are most often classified by many black folks as nerdy. They are many times called cornball - unless they are rap stars or movie stars and in the case of rap stars, they are many times called or classified as acting black. Now this is funny because black people from my understanding do not have any specialized way of acting. What some black people have been is what I like to call typecast. People mistakenly try to separate the things that black and white people do by cultural or geographical locations. They say that's a black thing – as with the rapping or that's a white thing – as with bungee jumping. But here's the bullshit: black and white people both do the same things. The only difference is that there is often a preponderance of certain things by a certain race, which causes that race to be speculated as the only ones that do it. On a Friday night, I have seen some black women dressed in skirts so small they could have been used as bras – and mind you, these women were wearing these items publicly. I guess that's why they got into some clubs and I didn't. On another Friday night, I can recall seeing white women wearing painfully small miniskirts, the likes of which, some strippers would not wear while performing their acts inside of a strip club. Does the fact that both races were degrading themselves by sometimes showing more ass than fabric matter? Of course not. I have seen both black men and white men, get pissy, sloppy drunk and stop traffic by either throwing up in the middle of the street from all of the alcohol or by engaging in a drunken brawl in an intersection. Does it make any race better than the other? No. What it does do is bring into focus the fact that people have hidden jealousies and biases against other races and will allow those biases to be exposed whenever someone of a different race does something that may seem questionable or uncouth to them. You ever hear someone say when a murder in the inner city is committed 'look at those minorities, animals – just animals?' or when somebody like Bernie Madoff rips off people for billions of dollars, someone saying 'white folks always doing that insider trading shit.' (Even though I believe he is Polish) Of course you have and the main reason why is because people want to believe that only black people do certain things and other people want to believe that only white people do certain other things.

Another ginormous perception when it comes to black folks and white folks is the one about blacks being better at sports just because they are black. Many people will argue that some of the best or most prolific basketball players in the past few years have been minorities. Some of the greatest baseball players have been minorities as well. Many of the greatest sports players in most major sports have been minorities. In fact, I think the only sport where there has not been a disproportionate level of minority dominance has been hockey. And one of the reasons why many people will fathom the reason as being is because hockey is not considered a 'black' sport. Now I am inclined to agree that many minorities have done extremely well in the area of sports over the last few decades but does that mean that they are genetically engineered to be better at sports just because they are black or could it be because they practice and train more than those of other races? Think about it for a second; if the above were actually true and not just speculation, wouldn't it be a wonderful thing for black people? Every black person would be able to make millions of dollars a year engaging in recreational activities just because they were black. But we all know that this is not true. What many people want to do is take what may be considered a little bit of truth and attach it to an entire race. The problem with this is that that little bit of truth will often define the entire race instead of just being something that a few ignorant people believe. Here are a couple of for instances: when people mention fried chicken and watermelon, the race which is historically and stereotypically connected to them is black, even though white people have been known to enjoy these things also. When people speak of college attendance or following in their parents' footsteps, the race which is connected to them is white, even though black people do attend and graduate college and even take over family businesses.

Perceptions are always going to cause controversy because they are almost never based on fact. They are based on either first or secondary impressions. The fact that people who make these perceptions regarding race do not fully explore them will continue to lead people into believing only what they initially see instead of the bigger picture.

On Professional Sports Teams

I am a sports fan. No, let me clarify, I am a diehard New York Yankee fan. I love almost everything about the game of baseball from the sound of the crack of the bat, as a home run is being hit to the excitement of hearing an arena full of screaming fans to just walking by Yankee Stadium. With that being said, I have never understood the need to pay millions and millions of dollars to certain players to play the sport. I do understand that it's not about just playing – it's about winning – why else would these sports organizations pay such exorbitant salaries? I mean it's a recreational activity for crying out loud. It is something that children do after school and on weekends. Kids don't do spreadsheets for recreation. Kids don't work in offices for forty or fifty hours a week either. Kids play. And they play not to relieve stress but because it's something that kids are expected to do. It is also something they enjoy. So why is it that people are paying those who attend college for years and years less than they are paying those who perform a recreational activity on a professional level? Do you see the hypocrisy? Here's a novel idea – why not do like many other jobs and pay based on performance? Give everybody a 100k to start, then if they win a series bump it up to a million dollar payout for each of the players on the team. That would definitely cause some rivalry or at least initiative. It would make the players work for their money instead of just playing in a lackadaisical manner. Think about something: most of these professional millionaires have never seen this much money before in their lives – even if they don't win a series, don't they still get to keep that money that they make during the year? Think about something else: these organizations are paying many times over one million per year to somebody who is used to making nowhere near that. Do you really think they're going to give their all every chance they get? If I knew I was gonna get a check as long as I showed up to work and did a job, not did a job well but just did a job, I would be there everyday with my lackadaisical ass. In addition to that, where is this money coming from? Thought we had a debt crisis? Funny how there's a so called crisis but yet there's always millions and millions to pay to baseball players and basketball players and football players. Is there some unending sports fund, which keeps billions and billions of dollars on standby just for those star players and star teams who reach the World Series or playoffs every year?

This is some of the bullshit that I try to wrap my head around. If professional players all had a starting salary of one hundred thousand dollars, there would be an almost astronomical amount of money set aside for other things that this nation and world so desperately needs. Think about all the players who normally would be worth $100 million dollars over five years or something like that. If they all only received $100k, those extra millions could be applied to the debt, which seems to never be decreasing. Those millions and millions could be geared toward the homeless situation that we have in this country. Combine all the money that could be saved from the sports salaries with the lottery nonsense, more specifically, their one, two and three hundred million dollar payouts and such – and there would be a surplus such as the world has never known. But the powers that be do not think with a mindset such as this. What they think is that this country needs sports more than food and shelter. They think that winning championships are more important than the basic needs of human beings. I think that's some real bullshit but my little opinion doesn't really matter now does it? If I could change things around, I would make it as such – focus on what everybody needs such as food, shelter and water. Then focus on things that people want such as baseball, basketball and football. A lot of people talk about how things are getting better but I'm am kinda perplexed – how is it that a baseball player can amass a million dollars per year, and the homeless guy panhandling outside the stadium does not have a dollar in his pocket? Is that what you call better? Maybe it's me but it seems like a lot of the priorities in this country are really fucked up.

On This Tipping Thing

A long time ago in a galaxy far, far away, there was a practice, which entailed giving money to those who performed a deed or service in addition to what the service or deed actually costs. That practice was called tipping. The reason behind the existence of tipping was originally designed to show one's appreciation for a very good service performed by another. **Now here comes the bullshit:** Tipping is no longer a random act based on how well a person or organization does a particular job or service. Now tipping is a mandatory gesture, which is not reasonably but forcibly expected and many times stolen. Now I know many of you may be asking how can one steal a tip. Well aside from the obvious walking by a table where the previous guests have left a tip, which the servers have yet to pick up and swiping it, there is this somewhat new process that many establishments have enacted which entails removing money without my permission. They call it a gratuity. I call it bullshit. I found out about this practice much by accident. My significant other and I were having dinner one time at a halfway decent restaurant and after the check came it came with some crazy shit. The tip had already been added to the bill! I thought to myself what kind of shit was that? I mean they didn't ask my permission. They didn't even inquire if we had enjoyed the meal but they in their infinite wisdom, graciously added a 15 or 18 or whatever the fuck it was tip to the price of dinner. I am so glad that I did not have that much to drink where I would have just doled out whatever the amount of the dinner was without taking a second look because normally I am the type of individual to leave a tip if the service is anywhere near decent. I would have been beyond pissed if I had done so. I mean can you imagine paying for dinner, paying an included tip which they cleverly include in what I believe to be very fine print on the ticket and then giving another tip because it's the right thing to do? That shit is crazy! My question is what if the service was lousy and I really had no intention of tipping? I guess this is one way lazy or inept employees sidestep this. According to this practice, there will be a tip given regardless to how well or how bad the service is. That's some bullshit. And on top of that, check out how some of these motherfuckers actually expect a tip on top of the taken out tip if they feel they go above and beyond what their job description actually is. I have been in establishments where after settling the bill, these individuals will bring back your change in singles and count them slowly, one by one, almost as if they expect you to get tired and just say it's okay you keep that. Not me. Call me a cheap motherfucker if you want but I do not understand the logic of how people can steal from you and one, not expect you to become upset behind the action and two, expect you to give the thieving bastards more money. Here's my thing: if a person is employed in the hospitality industry, then that person should be fucking hospitable. They should not do their job just because they think that they are going to get a tip. They should do it because of the plain and simple fact that it is what they are supposed to fucking do. I call the process of unauthorized money retrieval AKA tipping, stealing because when you take money from someone without their permission, it is called stealing. You can go to jail for that in any state in the union but as long as you are inside of a restaurant, those rules do not apply. When it is explained that way, it sounds a lot closer to bullshit, doesn't it? I agree, it does.

Well this brings us to the close of another titillating edition of the ramblings of Jeremiah Dotson. I sincerely hope you enjoyed it. This 9th edition, It's All Bullshit, was just a small list and explanation of some of the things in this world which I believe are a boatload of crap. I call this edition a small list because I know that it barely scratches the surface of what some of you may consider bullshit in this world and it may not even touch any of the bullshit lists that some of you may already have of your own. But never fear, as long as there is bullshit in this world to speak of, whether it is in the form of relationships, finances, government assistance programs or what have you, I will definitely speak on it in the most bullshit free way I know. Until next time – and oh yes, there will be a next time,

Jeremiah Dotson

P.S. If you have enjoyed this book, hated this book or just want to see what else I spend countless hours, days, weeks and months doing when I should be working, you can go to Amazon.com /Jeremiah Dotson or you can contact me at Facebook.com or Deceptive1@hotmail.com.

END